MAINSTREAMING HUMAN RIGHTS

in Whitehall and Westminster

Ian Bynoe and
Sarah Spencer

INSTITUTE FOR PUBLIC POLICY RESEARCH

INSTITUTE FOR PUBLIC POLICY RESEARCH

30-32 Southampton St
London WC2E 7RA
Tel: 0171 470 6100
Fax: 0171 470 6111
ippr@easynet.co.uk
www.ippr.org.uk
Registered charity 800065

The Institute for Public Policy Research is an independent charity whose purpose is to contribute to public understanding of social, economic and political questions through research, discussion and publication. It was established in 1988 by leading figures in the academic, business and trade-union communities to provide an alternative to the free market think tanks.

IPPR's research agenda reflects the challenges facing Britain and Europe. Current programmes cover the areas of economic and industrial policy, Europe, governmental reform, human rights, social policy, the environment and media issues.

Besides its programme of research and publication, IPPR also provides a forum for political and trade union leaders, academic experts and those from business, finance, government and the media, to meet and discuss issues of common concern.

Trustees

Production & design by **EMPHASIS**
ISBN 1 86030 074 X
© IPPR 1999
Printed and bound in Great Britain by
Biddles Ltd, Guildford and King's Lynn

Contents

Acknowledgements

The Institute for Public Policy Research wishes to thank the Nuffield Foundation for funding this research and the many organisations and individuals who helped in the course of the study, providing information and materials or agreeing to be interviewed. In particular, the authors thank Lord Lester QC, whose public lecture 'Taking Human Rights Seriously' in 1994 inspired IPPR to initiate the project; barrister Jonathan Cooper who contributed a considerable amount of research for the book and continued to advise on its policy content; Helena Cook, who conducted the initial research for the project; Francesca Klug who generously gave of her time to read and comment on drafts of the report; the civil servants who agreed to be interviewed and the experts in the field who attended a seminar on the research findings.

The views and proposals published in this report are those of the authors. They are not necessarily endorsed by the IPPR, its staff or trustees.

About the authors

Ian Bynoe is a full-time member of the Police Complaints Authority. A solicitor who has worked in law centres and in private practice, he was legal director of MIND from 1990-1994. His previous publications for the IPPR are: with Oliver M and Barnes C, *Equal rights for disabled people* (1991); *Beyond the Citizen's Charter* (1996); *Rights to fair treatment* (1997); and with Spencer S *A Human Rights Commission: the options for Britain and Northern Ireland* (1998).

Sarah Spencer is the Director of the Human Rights Programme at the IPPR and was formerly the General Secretary of the National Council for Civil Liberties. Her recent publications include, with Bynoe I, *A Human Rights Commission: the options for Britain and Northern Ireland* (1998); 'The impact of immigration policy on race relations' in Blackstone T (et al, eds) *Race relations in Britain* (Routledge 1998); series editor for a series of four publications on children's involvement in decision-making (1995-6) and *Strangers and Citizens, a positive approach to migrants and refugees* (ed) (IPPR 1994). Sarah Spencer is a Member of the Home Office Taskforce on implementation of the Human Rights Act.

Summary

The Human Rights Act 1998, incorporating the European Convention on Human Rights into UK domestic law, promises unprecedented change for the ways in which domestic public policy is shaped and legislation drafted – not only for the UK government but equally for devolved government in Scotland, Wales and Northern Ireland. The first priority will be to ensure that legislation, policy and practice comply with the Convention – to prevent breaches of the Human Rights Act – and the report sets out the reforms which will be necessary in Whitehall and in the UK Parliament to provide that assurance.

The report then argues that mere compliance, a risk management strategy, should not be the sole objective. It the government's aim is to promote good practice, to foster a 'culture of rights' throughout the public sector and the public at large, human rights objectives must be built into the heart of the legislative and policy making process.

Human Rights Act

The Human Rights Act requires government to ensure that legislation, policy and practice – or failure to act – comply with the rights and freedoms in the European Convention (ECHR). If it fails to do so, it can be challenged in the courts. The Act requires a Minister who is introducing a Bill to Parliament to state whether the Bill is compatible with the Convention. If a court finds a provision in primary legislation incompatible with the Convention, it will make a Declaration of Incompatibility. The government must then decide whether to amend the law through usual parliamentary procedures or through a fast-track Remedial Order. If a court finds any provision in secondary legislation to be incompatible, it will be able to declare that provision invalid.

Need for reform recognised

The Act thus requires changes in Whitehall procedures when preparing policy and legislation and in Parliamentary procedures for scrutinising legislation and Remedial Orders. This is recognised by the government and draft guidance for civil servants is in preparation. It was further announced in December 1998 that a Parliamentary Select Committee on Human Rights will be established in 1999 to conduct inquiries, scrutinise draft legislation and Remedial Orders and to consider whether there is a need for a separate Human Rights Commission.

This report considers in detail the changes needed in Whitehall and the role which the new parliamentary committee should play. While it focuses on Whitehall and Westminster, the case which it makes for mainstreaming human rights in policy development, and for the role of the parliamentary committee, are equally applicable to the newly devolved administrations in Scotland, Wales and Northern Ireland. The report's focus is a practical one: how the machinery of government and the conduct of parliamentary business can be adapted for incorporation. It builds on existing models and recognises that the procedures designed to deliver human rights standards have to be reconciled with the constraints of a busy legislative time-table.

International standards

The report describes the principal international human rights Conventions binding on the UK, including the ECHR, explaining the limitations at the international level for ensuring UK compliance. The limits of that system heighten the need for domestic machinery and procedures to ensure that the UK's commitments are respected, commitments which cover civil and political rights within the UK such as freedom from discrimination and freedom of speech, as well as socio-economic rights and the human rights of children.

Current Whitehall and Parliamentary procedures

The report then examines current procedures in Whitehall and in Westminster for ensuring compliance with those standards. It explains what scrutiny for compliance with international standards actually means – that it involves both legal and political judgements – and finds both Whitehall and Westminster procedures severely wanting. Even in the case of the ECHR, the concern for compliance has received low priority and in relation to wider international human rights standards the impact on policy development would appear to have been marginal.

In designing the new system of parliamentary scrutiny, the report argues that certain lessons can be learnt from examining debates on primary legislation in previous Parliaments where human rights issues have been raised: that Members have been unable to deploy sufficient expertise on international human rights law and the UK's obligations, unlike the government it having had no means to obtain expert legal advice; that inadequate time has been allocated for careful deliberation of the implications for human rights of particular provisions; that the lack of transparency of the 'Strasbourg proofing' process, and the absence of formal parliamentary procedures or institutions with a mandate to raise human rights issues have meant that Ministerial assurances have often gone unchallenged; and that the absence of any all-party focus for such scrutiny has meant that the task of raising human rights implications has fallen to opposition parties, creating the impression that human rights questions are party political rather than the responsibility of the whole House. Future arrangements need to equip members with expert advice and assistance to ensure that informed opinions on compliance with international standards – whether on proposed or existing legislation – carry greater authority.

A new approach

Looking to the future, the report argues that the new procedures in Whitehall and Westminster should be designed to achieve three principal objectives:

- to ensure compliance of law, policy and practice with the standards in the European Convention, to avoid challenge under the Human Rights Act; and to ensure domestic compliance with wider international human rights Conventions binding on the UK;

- to promote good practice throughout the public sector;

- to identify opportunities in policy and legislation to extend human rights protection and to promote greater respect for human rights and the responsibilities they entail.

In order to achieve these objectives, the report argues that scrutiny needs to become a more proactive process, capable of influencing the development of policy, procedures and law earlier in their design and drafting. The emphasis within the scrutiny process must shift from a focus solely on prevention and the avoidance of risk to a goal-oriented process which reflects the government's responsibility to guarantee the body of international human rights standards to all of its citizens, and its desire to promote a culture of rights and responsibilities. To that end, government should draw on parallel initiatives which have been established to achieve comparable goals across government departments. The Policy Assessment and Fair Treatment procedures in Northern Ireland, environmental impact assessments, the greening government initiative and the Better Regulation Unit (now Regulatory Impact Unit) are given as examples.

Scrutiny must involve a significant level of expertise, providing decision makers with timely, accurate and relevant information on issues of compliance and good practice; and the process should be more transparent, reflecting Ministers' desire to promote a new culture of openness. Elected representatives and the public will then be able to assess the reasons for decisions. Procedures must be seen to be more rigorous and systematic with clearer outcomes, some of which can be evaluated. They must not be restricted to assessing the impact of existing proposals but identify new opportunities to extend human rights protection and awareness. Finally, changes in procedures must be practical and viable.

Reform in Whitehall

Drawing on existing experience of impact assessments within Whitehall and Northern Ireland government departments, on the innovative cross-government machinery introduced by the current government, and on experience abroad, the report recommends the following approach to put human rights at the heart of government decision-making:

Cabinet Office guidance on Human Rights Impact Assessments

Guidance would cover compliance and promotion of good practice in relation to the ECHR and to wider international human rights standards. It would be used in relation to all proposed policy and legislation as well as, selectively, to assess compliance of existing legislation and policy. The relationship between Human Rights Impact Assessments and the existing, little known procedures in Whitehall for *Policy Appraisal for Equal Treatment*, should be considered.

Leadership at Ministerial level

A Minister, supported by a central unit, should be given responsibility for ensuring that this policy is implemented effectively across government. The unit should be tasked with ensuring that human rights impact assessments consider both compliance and good practice and are attached to all policy and legislative proposals seeking collective government approval. The unit should also be responsible for developing proposals for a cross-government human rights strategy, drawing on and responding to proposals coming from each department. It should compile an annual Human Rights Report on human rights in domestic policy, mirroring that prepared by the Foreign and Commonwealth Office on human rights in foreign policy. The report should be presented to Parliament and examined by the Human Rights Committee.

A Minister within each department should be given responsibility for ensuring that his or her department implements the approach effectively, ensuring that there is a structure in place at official level to deliver the dual objectives of scrutiny for compliance and the achievement of positive human rights objectives.

Annual report

Each department should report to the central human rights unit on the impact of the department's initiatives on human rights during the year and the steps taken by the department to promote human rights. That information should include a summary of the reasoning behind any s.19 statements on Bills and should be covered in each department's annual report.

Human rights manual

A comprehensive manual should be circulated to all government departments and agencies explaining the international human rights standards, how they are enforced at the international level and how they can be used to develop better policy and practice within in the UK. The manual would complement the more detailed Cabinet Office guidance relating to the European Convention, and would be the principal means of ensuring that policy and practice reflect the UK's international obligations on civil, political, socio-economic and cultural rights within the UK.

Reform in Westminster

Primary responsibility for enhancing Parliament's role in promoting human rights scrutiny and accountability will fall on the new joint Human Rights Committee. It should fulfil the following functions:

Scrutiny of primary legislation

Each Bill should be accompanied by a summary of the results of its Human Rights Impact Assessment. It would pinpoint any provisions in the Bill which could breach the ECHR or wider international standards, and the government's position in relation to those concerns: either that, on balance, no breach would follow from the provision or why the government wishes to proceed with the legislation nevertheless. On the rare occasions when the Bill includes a 'nevertheless statement', additional procedural rules are recommended. Initial scrutiny would in practice be conducted by the Committee's expert staff who would draw Members' attention to any provision meriting their attention. A key question will be whether the Committee will receive a copy of the Bill in time to consider it and, if necessary, to take evidence from outside experts, prior to the Bill having its Second Reading or Committee stage.

Remedial Orders

To consider government proposals for Remedial Orders following a Declaration of Incompatibility under the Human Rights Act or an adverse ruling from the European Court of Human Rights. No Order should be put to Parliament for an affirmative resolution until the Committee has had an opportunity to consider it.

Scrutiny of delegated legislation

To advise whether any provision in proposed delegated legislation is incompatible with the European Convention.

Monitoring existing policy and practice

Following the practice of departmental Select Committees, the Human Rights Committee should conduct inquiries into existing legislation and policy, using the ECHR and wider international human rights standards as its yardstick. The Committee could inquire into aspects of policy causing serious public concern and should have the flexibility to conduct an urgent investigation into a severe or systemic abuse of human rights. On other occasions, it could take an international standard (such as the UN Convention on the Rights of the Child) as its starting point and take evidence on UK compliance with its obligations under that Convention. The timing of such an inquiry could mirror that of the UN reporting system on the Convention in question. The Committee could have a close relationship with non-departmental public bodies working in the human rights field such as the Commission for Racial Equality and the Data Protection Registrar, seeking their advice where appropriate and questioning them on their work and priorities.

The Committee should complement the work of departmental Select Committees and scrutiny committees, avoiding duplication of effort through liaison through the appropriate channels.

Involvement in treaty ratification and reports to UN supervisory bodies

Parliament is currently permitted only a minimal role in the treaty making process. Its approval was not sought, nor any debate held, when the ECHR was ratified in 1950, nor when the UN's equivalent Convention, the ICCPR, was ratified in 1976. Parliament is equally excluded when government decides to derogate from a human rights treaty or enter reservations. The report proposes a consultative role for the Committee during the negotiation and ratification process, raising the option of a more formal decision-making procedure.

Under the key international human rights Conventions, the government must report on progress to the UN on a regular basis, usually every three or five years.*Mainstreaming Human Rights* recommends that the Human Rights Committee should be aware of, and sometimes be involved in, that process. It could conduct its own inquiry into compliance with the Convention, for instance the

Convention on the Elimination of Racial Discrimination; or question Ministers on issues of concern raised by the UN supervisory body.

Raising public awareness of human rights

The government has suggested that the Committee could play a role in raising public understanding and respect for human rights and awareness of the Human Rights Act in particular. It is unrealistic to expect a Parliamentary Committee to make a major contribution in this key area. It could, however, monitor the attempts made by government and others to do so, a task on which the government is currently advised by a Home Office Task Force.

Structure and status of the Committee

The Human Rights Committee will be composed of members of both Houses of Parliament. Whether its chair is drawn from the House of Lords or Commons, from the opposition or the governing party, it is vital that the Committee be robustly independent. A committee which felt constrained to support the government on each controversial issue would not serve the public well. In order to scrutinise policy and legislation effectively, it will be *essential* for the Committee to have regular access to expert legal opinion, in particular expertise on international human rights jurisprudence.

On some issues, it will be necessary for the Committee to take evidence from individuals or groups adversely or beneficially affected by proposed legislation in order to assess whether that legislation is proportional to the problem it is addressing and 'necessary in a democratic society', as required by the terms of the Human Rights Act. As the government has suggested, it may therefore by necessary for the Committee to conduct hearings in other parts of the country, to gain a clear perspective on the relevant social, moral and ethical issues.

The Committee will need the powers enjoyed by other Select Committees including the power to send for persons, papers and records. It would be assisted significantly were a Human Rights Commission established in Britain, as has recently been established in Northern Ireland. Among other roles, it advises the Northern Ireland Assembly and scrutinises draft legislation.

If the reforms advocated in this report are implemented, the government and Parliament will have taken a major step towards ensuring not only that the UK complies with its international human rights obligations but that human rights, and recognition of the responsibilities which they entail, are built into the heart of the policy-making process.

Key recommendations

- Human Rights Impact Assessments on policy and legislative proposals

- Objective: to promote good practice, not merely to ensure compliance with the Human Rights Act

- New central Human Rights Unit to coordinate approach across government, reporting to senior Minister

- Ministerial champion within each department to ensure procedures implemented effectively

- Annual human rights report, mirroring FCO report on human rights in foreign policy

- Robust, independent Parliamentary Select Committee on Human Rights to:
  - Conduct inquiries into serious or systemic human rights issues
  - Inquire into UK compliance with its international human rights obligations, eg on race equality or the human rights of children, within the UK
  - Scrutinise proposed legislation
  - Consider the government's response to legislation declared by the courts to be incompatible with the European Convention on Human Rights
  - Be consulted when the UK is negotiating or ratifying an international human rights treaty

1. A new era for human rights

The United Kingdom is about to embark on a process of unparalleled importance for the practice of government and the formulation of law and policy. During the year 2000, the Human Rights Act 1998 will come fully into force, giving effect within UK domestic law to the rights in the European Convention on Human Rights (ECHR). This single measure promises unprecedented change for the ways in which public policy is shaped and legislation is drafted.

This report considers the reforms which will be necessary in Whitehall and in Parliament in order to ensure that legislation, policy and practice comply with the Convention and thus avoid challenge in the courts. It then considers whether mere *compliance* with the Convention will be sufficient to achieve the Government's objective: that the Act lead to a 'culture of human rights' both within the public sector and among the public at large. We shall argue that, to achieve that goal, human rights objectives will have to be built into the heart of the legislative and policy-making process. While the report focuses on Whitehall and Westminster, the approach it sets out is equally applicable to the Scottish Executive and Parliament and to the Northern Ireland and Welsh Assemblies.

Human Rights Act 1998

The Act repositions the European Convention closer to the centre of UK politics. It requires that government, all public authorities, and private bodies which fulfil public functions, ensure that they comply with the Convention. Home Office Minister Lord Williams of Mostyn confidently told Parliament that:

> Every public authority will know that its behaviour, its structures, its conclusions and its executive actions will be subject to this (human rights) culture.[1]

The Act enables any individual who believes that their rights under the Convention have been infringed to seek a remedy in the courts. They may also raise Convention principles in any proceedings taken by, or against, public authorities.

If judges believe that any provision in secondary legislation breaches the Convention, they will be able to declare that provision invalid. If they consider that a provision in primary legislation is incompatible, they cannot strike it down but may make a Declaration of Incompatibility.[2] When this happens, Ministers must consider whether or not to amend the law and whether to use a fast-track Remedial Order procedure to do so.[3] The approval of both Houses of Parliament will be necessary for such an Order, except in exceptional circumstances. In the normal course of events, when the government decides to amend the law to bring it into line with the judges' ruling, it will do so through the usual legislative procedure. The provision in the Act for a fast-track procedure, however, effectively requires Parliament to introduce a procedure for consideration of such Remedial Orders.

S.19 of the Act, which has already come into force,[4] similarly requires procedural reform. S.19 requires each Minister, when introducing any Bill in Parliament, to state whether the Bill complies with the standards in the Convention or whether, despite the fact that it may not do so, the government nevertheless wishes Parliament to enact it. The statement is to be printed on the face of the Bill, each provision of which must thus be carefully scrutinised for compatibility with the Convention, to enable the Minister to make the required statement.

Implementation

The government recognises that significant changes will be needed both in Whitehall and in Parliament in order to prevent breaches of the Convention. When introducing the Human Rights Bill in 1997, Lord Irvine of Lairg, the Lord Chancellor said:

> ...there will have to be close scrutiny of the human rights implications of all legislation before it goes forward.[5]

and the Home Secretary told Parliament in October 1998 that the government is:

> ...ensuring that government departments and other public

authorities are properly prepared for the obligations that the Bill places on them. They will need not only to review their legislation and practices for compatibility with the Convention but to ensure that their staff are trained in an awareness of the Convention rights so that those rights permeate all the decisions that they take' [6]

When in opposition, the Labour Party had set out its plans to incorporate the Convention in a consultation paper, *Bringing Rights Home*. It suggested that a new Joint Committee of both Houses of Parliament could be established to monitor how incorporation was working, to conduct inquiries and, perhaps, to have a role in the scrutiny of draft legislation. There would be a need, it recognised, not only for Whitehall but for Parliament to scrutinise new legislation, and ensure the conformity of law with human rights obligations under international treaties.[7]

The idea of a new Parliamentary committee was reiterated in the government's subsequent White Paper, *Rights Brought Home*, published with the Human Rights Bill in October 1997. It argued that it would be:

highly desirable for the government to ensure as far as possible that legislation which it places before Parliament in the normal way is compatible with the Convention rights, and for Parliament to ensure that the human rights implications of legislation are subject to proper consideration before the legislation is enacted.[8]

The new committee, it suggested,

might conduct enquiries on a range of human rights issues relating to the Convention, and produce reports so as to assist the government and Parliament in deciding what action to take. It might also want to range more widely, and examine issues relating to the other international obligations of the United Kingdom such as proposals to accept new rights under other human rights treaties.[9]

The Act thus creates an opportunity, and effectively requires, human rights standards to become an integral part of the legislative and policy making process. Draft guidance to civil servants is in preparation by the Cabinet Office and a Home Office Task Force began work in January 1999 to help ensure that Whitehall and public authorities prepare for the Act coming into force.

In December 1998 it was confirmed that a Human Rights Committee will be established in the Summer of 1999 as a joint committee of both Houses of Parliament, to begin work in the Autumn. Its terms of reference have not yet been agreed but are to include the conduct of inquiries into human rights issues, scrutiny of Remedial Orders under the Human Rights Act, examining draft legislation for compatibility with the Convention, and considering whether Britain needs a Human Rights Commission to monitor the Act.[10]

In establishing such a committee, Parliament will be following an international trend. The national parliaments of 52 countries already have a committee or sub-committee with responsibility for human rights issues; in a further 44 countries human rights are part of a broader remit such as constitutional affairs.[11] This report considers the potential contribution which a parliamentary Human Rights Committee could make in the UK, both in relation to monitoring the Human Rights Act and, as the government has suggested, to wider human rights issues.

Devolution

The need for human rights to be built into the legislative and policy process will not be restricted to Whitehall and Westminster. The devolved Executive and Parliament in Scotland, which will have extensive legislative responsibility, and the Assembly in Wales, will also have to ensure that their actions (and failure to act) comply with the Convention. They will thus similarly be required to introduce scrutiny procedures. Where they fail to comply with the Convention, the courts will be able nullify their decisions.

The relevant provisions are contained in the Scotland Act 1998 and the Government of Wales Act 1998 which will come into force when the Parliament and Assembly are established in 1999, prior to the Human Rights Act itself coming into force in the year 2000. On or before the introduction of a Bill in the Scottish Parliament, a member of the Scottish Executive must confirm that in their view its provisions are within the Parliament's legislative competence, including confirmation that it is compatible with the Convention. Scottish office guidance confirms that:

> This will require officials and their lawyers to consider the impact of legislative proposals on Convention rights in the drafting process.[12]

The guidance states that:

> The Scotland Act and the Human Rights Act, taken together, represent a major step forward in building a modern and effective human rights culture in Scotland.

The Scottish office of Amnesty International UK, arguing that the creation of the Scottish Parliament creates an historic opportunity to review the protection of human rights in Scotland, has similarly recognised the need for human rights impact assessments to ensure that proposed legislation and policy do not infringe the Convention:

> The establishment of a Human Rights Unit in the Scottish Administration, with representation across departments, might enable this duty of the First Minister and the Executive to be discharged effectively. Such a unit does not preclude the 'mainstreaming' of human rights across all departments, but would serve to ensure that human rights standards and treaties were considered effectively by all departments.[13]

Northern Ireland Act 1998

Changes now due in Northern Ireland, following the Good Friday Agreement and election of the new Assembly, are likely to prove the most far reaching in their effect on human rights – with lessons for the rest of the UK. The elected Assembly will have devolved law-making powers, in the exercise of which it will have to comply with the ECHR.

As in Scotland, any measures which breach the rights in the Convention can be struck down by the courts. To assist the Assembly to ensure that its actions do comply, however, it will be required by s.13 of the Northern Ireland Act to send a copy of each Bill to the newly-established Human Rights Commission.

The functions of the Commission include:[14]

- advising the Assembly whether a Bill is compatible with 'human rights'. Human rights 'includes' the rights in the ECHR;

- keeping under review the adequacy and effectiveness in Northern Ireland of law and practice relating to the protection of human rights;

- advising the Secretary of State, and the Assembly's Executive Committee, of legislative and other measures which ought to be taken to protect human rights.

The possibility of establishing a Human Rights Commission in Britain was included in the Labour Party's pre-election consultation paper, *Bringing Rights Home*. Provision for such a body was not included in the Human Rights Bill although the government has not closed its mind to doing so at a later date. The Parliamentary Human Rights Committee will conduct an enquiry into whether such a body is needed.[15] The case for a Human Rights Commission and what it might achieve is developed in greater detail in IPPR's report *A Human Rights Commission: the options for Britain and Northern Ireland.*[16]

Earlier proposals for reform

It is only the introduction of the Human Rights Act which has led to acceptance of the need for improved human rights scrutiny in Whitehall and Westminster. It will be welcomed by those who have consistently argued the need for this reform, proposing the kind of Parliamentary scrutiny which is now to be introduced. This report, like the government's own approach, has been much influenced by the case which they made.

In the main, previous proposals have been associated with the Liberal Democrat lawyer, Lord Lester of Herne Hill. In his maiden speech in 1993[17] he advocated the appointment by the Lords of a new Select

Committee to examine Bills and to report whether any of their provisions appeared to be inconsistent with the UK's obligations under the ECHR or the UN's equivalent instrument – the International Covenant on Civil and Political Rights. Shortly after this, four eminent legal peers from all parties, including the current Lord Chancellor, Lord Irvine, signed a Memorandum[18] urging the Liaison Committee of the House of Lords to add scrutiny of Bills for compatibility with the ECHR to the then functions of the Delegated Powers Scrutiny Committee. They argued that Parliament had passed legislation which proved in the fullness of time to be incompatible with the ECHR. It had not done so deliberately:

> but because neither House of Parliament has the machinery or the appropriate procedures to take the obligations of the Convention systematically into account in the course of its legislative work.

The Memorandum neatly summarised what would be involved in the first stage scrutiny function. It stressed that such scrutiny should only be concerned:

> ...with reporting, on the basis of evidence and legal advice, whether the Bill concerned did or did not comply with the Convention. It would not be concerned with the political merits of the proposed legislation, and there would be no need or, indeed, time available for lengthy or discursive reports.

This attempt to expand the role of the Committee was unsuccessful.

Lord Lester's 1996 Private Member's Bill to incorporate the Convention into UK law[19] included a procedure requiring Ministers, when introducing Bills in Parliament, to explain why any provision was or appeared to be inconsistent with the requirements of the ECHR. The procedure found in the Human Rights Act closely resembles Lord Lester's.

The UK's record at Strasbourg

Peers' concern that Parliament should exercise more effective control over proposed legislation, to ensure its compliance with the ECHR, was prompted in part by the number of cases taken against the UK to the

European Court of Human Rights in Strasbourg. The UK government had, by April 1999, been found to have breached the ECHR on 52 occasions.

In this growing list of cases the areas of law, policy and administration judged to have breached Convention standards include a wide range of subjects including the restriction of prisoners' civil rights; corporal punishment in state schools; discriminatory immigration rules; ministerial control of the release of detained psychiatric patients and life prisoners; telephone tapping by an employer; refusing access to social services records; denying legal aid to those at risk of imprisonment for non-payment of fines; providing inadequate legal protection for journalists required to reveal a source; employing unfair court martial procedures to enforce military discipline; introducing retrospective criminal penalties and failing to guarantee respect for human life. In a number of cases, the breach occurred because of provisions in primary and secondary legislation. In a number of other cases, the breach occurred because of the absence of legislation to prevent it.

UK foreign policy

Developments in UK foreign policy, and a higher profile for human rights within it, provide added impetus to the changes needed in Whitehall and Westminster. A comprehensive review of the UK's human rights obligations is underway. In addition, officials are examining those treaty provisions which have not yet been fully accepted. A warmer relationship is evident between the UK and the Council of Europe, particularly concerning the Council's programme for reform of the Court of Human Rights.

A human rights dimension to Labour policy abroad is far from unprecedented. UK governments, particularly those of Attlee (1945-51) and Wilson (1964-1970 and 1974-1976), played a leading role in the post war development of international human rights treaties both within the United Nations and the Council of Europe. They ratified many significant instruments drafted by these organisations, setting minimum human rights standards across a wide range of civil, political, social and cultural activities.

If the current government's approach to human rights in foreign policy is sustained, it cannot fail to have some impact on domestic policy. As explicit human rights standards are given greater prominence abroad, this will highlight their relatively lower profile at home, unless changes are introduced which give them greater priority. At the least, it will increase the need for government to be able to demonstrate that its domestic policies and conduct adhere scrupulously to the standards it demands that other countries should meet.

The issues

The Human Rights Act promises greater openness by government when it deals with human rights issues and of Ministers being held to account more effectively for their actions, policies and proposals when these are judged against Convention standards.

The courts will, of course, play a critical role in holding the government and public authorities to account for what they do – or do not do – if the rights in the Convention have been breached. But it is the responsibility of the Executive and of Parliament to seek to prevent such breaches. This, at least, is their first responsibility.

When bringing the Human Rights Act into force, the government faces a choice. Ministers could limit their response to enhancing scrutiny procedures so that proposals for new laws or fresh policies comply with the ECHR. The object of the new procedures would then be to avoid the possibility of challenge in the courts – *a risk management strategy.*

Ministers have, however, said that their objective is not solely to achieve compliance but to foster a culture of human rights throughout the public service and the public at large.[20] Rather than introduce procedures designed merely to ensure compliance, therefore, they could seek to ensure that positive steps are taken to promote that culture. Strong, cross-government machinery and procedures have been introduced to ensure good practice and consistency in achieving other government objectives. Mechanisms to mainstream equality objectives in Northern Ireland, to ensure that government policies and services contribute towards environmental protection, and that they do not impose unnecessary regulation on business, are apt examples. Procedures could similarly be introduced to mainstream human rights objectives within the legislative and policy-making process.

At the time the Human Rights Bill was introduced, the government rejected the idea that it might give a Minister, backed by a central unit, the task of ensuring compliance across government.[21] That, however, was in October 1997, before it became clear how concerted the effort would need to be across Whitehall to ensure compliance by existing as well as future legislation, and before cross-cutting Ministerial initiatives became a familiar sight in other policy areas.

Finally, rather than defining human rights solely as those rights in the European Convention, the government's and Parliament's approach could embrace those wider human rights standards found in later international instruments also binding on the UK, such as the UN Convention on the Rights of the Child. It is often forgotten that the UK's international commitments are not limited to the basic standards found in the ECHR. During the past 50 years, UK governments have ratified a series of important UN treaties concerning civil and political rights, equality rights and the rights of children. It recently ratified a new Council of Europe Framework Convention on the rights of national minorities.

The widely-applicable provisions of these conventions may now acquire a fresh significance for the courts, which are expected to draw on them to assist in interpreting the ECHR, and for a government determined to respect the commitments it has made at the international level. The government has itself suggested that the Parliamentary Human Rights Committee should not restrict itself to monitoring ECHR compliance but take a role in relation to the UK's wider commitments. This report considers what form that role might take.

Currently, Parliament is not involved at all in the process of negotiation leading to the agreement of a human rights treaty and its subsequent ratification. Nor does it play any formal role in monitoring the UK's compliance with its international obligations – such as those under the UN Conventions. In this report, we propose ways in which Parliament could have a say in those decisions and, in return, how those instruments could have a greater impact on policy and practice within the UK.

This report

This report sets out the options open to Whitehall and Westminster and some lessons which can be learned from the approaches adopted in the past. The government recognises that its own and Parliament's standards of scrutiny and accountability must improve if they are to meet the demands of incorporation. We describe, first, how this could be achieved; then, the further measures which could be adopted to foster a culture of rights throughout central government, to maximise the impact of the Act.

The report's focus is a practical one – how the machinery of government and the conduct of parliamentary business can be adapted for incorporation. It seeks to draw out the rationale for the new procedures, arguing that a clear goal should be identified before the procedure is designed to achieve it. It builds on existing models, recognising that it is easier to adapt and improve than to create anew. And it recognises that the need for procedures designed to deliver human rights standards have to be reconciled with the constraints of a busy legislative timetable.

After this introduction, the report is arranged in three chapters. Chapter 2 describes the current framework of human rights conventions and the standards which apply to the UK. Chapter 3 defines what is meant by scrutiny for compliance with human rights standards and then examines current practice in Whitehall and Parliament. We show that human rights have had a limited but recognised profile in Whitehall's administrative machinery, whilst at Westminster their distinct importance has hardly been formally registered. We assess the consequences of this neglect for the law, the political process, and the interests of the wider public.

Chapter 4 sets out our proposals for reform. Beginning with the principles which should guide future changes to procedure and practice, it outlines a programme of reforms in Whitehall and Westminster designed to raise standards of scrutiny and accountability to meet the policy aims we have identified.

The UK's international human rights commitments provide the starting point for this report and its context. The next chapter describes them and explains their significance.

Endnotes

1.   Second Reading Human Rights Bill, 3 November 1997, HL col 1308.
2.   Section 4, Human Rights Act 1998.

3. Sections 10-12, Human Rights Act 1998.

4   S.19 came into force on 24 November 1998.

5. Speaking in the House of Lords Second Reading Debate on the Human Rights Bill, Official Report 3 November 1997, col 1228.

6. Third Reading of the Human Rights Bill, House of Commons, 21 October 1998, col 1359.

7. Straw J and Boateng P (December 1996) *Bringing rights home: Labour's plans to incorporate the European Convention on Human Rights into UK law* Labour Party.

8. Home Office (1997) *Rights brought home: the Human Rights Bill* CM 3782 TSO paragraph 3.1.

9. Ibid, paragraph 3.7.

10. Leader of the House Margaret Beckett, Written Answer, 14 December 1998, col 603.

11. According to a survey conducted by the Inter-Parliamentary Union *World Directory of Parliamentary Human Rights Bodies* IPU 1993; quoted in Blackburn R and Plant R (eds), *Constitutional Reform: the Labour government's constitutional reform agenda* Longman 1999.

12. *Human Rights in Scotland: the European Convention on Human Rights, the Scotland Act and the Human Rights Act – guidance to officials* (1999)

13. *Human Rights and the Scottish Parliament* Amnesty International UK, 5 March 1999.

14. See Multi-party Agreement of 10 April 1998 (Command Paper 3883) and S.69 Northern Ireland Act.

15. Announced by the Leader of the House as one of the functions of the committee. Written Answer, 14 December 1998, col 603.

16. Spencer S and Bynoe I (1998) *A Human Rights Commission: the options for Britain and Northern Ireland* IPPR.

17. Lord Lester returned to this theme in his 1994 Paul Sieghart Memorial Lecture. See Lord Lester of Herne Hill 'Taking Human Rights Seriously' (1994-1995) *King's College Law Journal* Vol 5, 23 November 1993, HL Vol 550, col 169.

18. *Scrutiny of Legislation for Consistency with Obligations under the ECHR – a memorandum* signed by Lords Simon of Glaisdale, Alexander of Weedon, Irvine of Lairg and Lester of Herne Hill.

19. Human Rights Bill, Parliamentary Session 1996-97 HL Bill 11.

20. 'Incorporation of the Convention is going to operate as a very

substantial culture change. We want it to percolate into the workings of all the courts. We want a human rights culture to develop throughout society.' Lord Irvine of Lairg, the Lord Chancellor on Radio 4 *Analysis* 6 November 1997.

20. see *Rights Brought Home op cit.*

2. International obligations

A wide range of international human rights standards apply to the
business of government and law making in the United Kingdom. This
chapter outlines the most significant human rights treaties binding on
the UK, and the nature of the commitments which the UK has made, in
order to demonstrate why it is necessary for government and parliament
to have procedures which ensure the compliance of UK law and practice
with those international obligations.

The first modern international agreements on human rights sprang
from the world's reaction to the horrors of war, state terror and the
mass killings in Europe and beyond during the late 1930s and 1940s.
The UN's Universal Declaration of Human Rights and the Council of
Europe's European Convention on Human Rights (ECHR) were drafted
to address the desire of nations that such conditions should never again
occur.

More recent agreements, such as the UN Convention on the Rights
of the Child (UNCRC), reflect consensus that there remains a need to
develop international legal norms to protect the vulnerable and to
promote standards of behaviour appropriate to the late 20th century.
The UK government's decision to incorporate the ECHR through the
Human Rights Act, and to establish a Human Rights Commission in
Northern Ireland with a mandate extending to wider international
standards, demonstrates its recognition that there is a need to give
greater authority to these legal norms within the UK.

While the first aim of these treaties is to regulate the treatment of
individuals by their government (and, in the case of the UNCRC, also
the treatment of children by their parents and others), it was also overtly
stated that the intention was to ensure respect for human rights by every
individual and organisation. Thus the Universal Declaration of Human
Rights, whose 50th anniversary was celebrated in 1998, proclaimed
the Declaration as:

> a common standard of achievement for all peoples and all
> nations, to the end that every individual and every organ of
> society, keeping this Declaration constantly in mind, shall
> strive by teaching and education to promote respect for these
> rights and freedoms.

In ratifying these international instruments, states agree to ensure to all individuals the rights in the agreement. Thus Article 2 of the UN's International Covenant on Civil and Political Rights, one of the key instruments binding on the UK, commits states to:

> adopt such legislative or other measures as may be necessary to give effect to (those) rights

and Article 1 of the ECHR commits states to:

> secure to everyone within their jurisdiction the rights and freedoms defined in...this Convention.[1]

It is thus clear that, in ratifying the international human rights Conventions, the UK has committed itself to ensure, first, that it introduces the necessary measures to comply with the Convention; second, that it does not introduce measures which breach the Convention; and, third, that it ensures that the public are made aware of the principles which the government has undertaken both to promote and to uphold.

International human rights standards

The matrix of post war international human rights instruments is complex. Some are legally binding treaties accompanied by international supervisory and enforcement procedures. Others are published norms which may guide UK practice but which are not monitored internationally. In addition, Resolutions and Recommendations, adopted by the political organs of international organisations, may also set standards and guidelines for government behaviour but are of merely persuasive value.

Taken together, these instruments cover a wide spectrum of political and social activity in both the public and private spheres. They include religious, racial and sex discrimination, the rights of children, the treatment of detainees in prison and hospital, the rights of workers, and principles of political freedom, personal security, privacy, health, welfare and participation in public and political life.

Where a government has made a formal commitment to comply with an international human rights instrument, it is under an obligation to do so regardless of the effectiveness of any international supervisory mechanism which has been established to ensure compliance. In practice, the extent to which these diverse instruments do influence legislation and policy differ widely, depending on their subject matter and legal status. Indeed, with the exception of the ECHR, the substance and significance of many of these treaties is little known, even amongst those working in relevant fields.

We describe below a few of the key instruments binding on the UK and the limitations of the international system for monitoring and enforcing those treaties. The limitations of that system heighten the need for domestic machinery and procedures to ensure that the UK's commitments are respected.

In this report we focus on the principal human rights treaties which have been ratified by, and which are therefore binding on, the UK. They cover civil, political, social, economic and cultural rights and have a supervisory mechanism at the international level to oversee their full implementation. In the case of social, economic and cultural rights, however, enforcement can call for different approaches not strictly comparable to those required for justiciable human rights standards – there is, as a general rule, no individual complaints investigation machinery.

The lack of effective enforcement machinery at the international level heightens the importance of procedures at the national level to *monitor* compliance with those obligations, if the commitment is to amount to more than ratification on paper. In that context, and of particular relevance to this report, a recent recommendation of the UN committee which monitors compliance with the UN Convention on Economic, Social and Cultural Rights is significant:

> The Committee recommends that consideration be given to the requirement that a Human Rights Impact Assessment or Impact Statement be made an integral part of every proposed legislation or policy initiative on a basis analogous to Environmental Impact Assessments or Statements.[2]

In many countries, treaty obligations, binding in international law, also form part of the *domestic* law of that country and are enforceable at the national level. The UK's approach differs from this. Our government does not usually ratify a treaty unless and until it considers that UK domestic laws comply with its provisions. But it does not normally transfer international treaties into domestic law through primary legislation. Thus, with the exception of the ECHR, brought into UK law by the Human Rights Act 1998, none of the Council of Europe or UN treaties which we describe below has the status of UK law. They cannot, therefore, be directly enforced in the courts and tribunals of this country.

Most international bodies promoting such agreements permit individual states to modify the treaty to meet the particular circumstances of domestic law or institutions. Such departures from the text of conventions, or interpretations on their meaning for a particular country, are expressed as 'reservations' to the treaty. Reservations can only be declared when the treaty is ratified by the state in question. We describe below the UK's reservations to the principal Conventions.

In very limited circumstances, arising in times of war or civil emergency, a state may also be permitted, after it has ratified an agreement, to derogate from specific obligations which it contains. Our summary also indicates where the UK has notified such derogations. The right to enter reservations and to derogate from such agreements raises the question whether Parliament should have any influence on the decision by the government to do so, an issue to which we return.

Interpreting human rights standards

Human rights law differs from the approach usually taken in UK domestic law in a number of important respects. Some provisions, such as the ECHR prohibition against slavery, are expressed in specific and unambiguous terms, as in domestic law. Other principles, such as that protecting freedom of expression, are defined in a more general way and require purposive interpretation to fit the circumstances of the situation at issue. For the latter, the process of adjudication in the courts will involve a greater consideration of public policy factors and social reality than is normally the case.

Human rights standards are living instruments. They develop over time as public expectations of respect for individual choice and freedom change. The level of commitment to certain rights and their enforcement may involve distinctive approaches linked to the culture and society of a particular treaty nation. International law has evolved principles which preserve a degree of freedom for nations to choose how they will respect rights, permitting some variations to take account of national traditions and mores. The European Court of Human Rights, for example, has developed the principle of 'the margin of appreciation' to allow for local adaptation.[3]

Furthermore, the exercise of one right may compete with another. The exercise of the right to freedom of expression, for example, may clash with the right to privacy. The role of human rights instruments, then, is often not to say definitively whether certain actions are to be permitted but to provide a framework within which the application of potentially conflicting rights can be assessed and determined.

In view of this, it is hard to escape the conclusion that, for human rights to be respected and enforced, not only legal but ethical and political positions must be explicitly adopted and justified. This points to the need for the involvement of elected representatives in assessing compliance with international standards as well as the need, as in the case of the Human Rights Act, for a judicial mechanism.

Council of Europe treaties

As a member of the Council of Europe the UK is party to a number of important regional human rights treaties, including the ECHR.

The European Convention on Human Rights

The ECHR, ratified by the UK in March 1951, came into force on 3 September 1953. Since that time, it has become the main source of human rights principles across Europe, particularly since the creation of the European Court of Human Rights in 1959. Its case law has been adopted around the world. By 1998, 40 member states of the Council of Europe had ratified it, agreeing to be subject to the jurisdiction of the Court.

The rights which it provides are wide ranging, albeit that there are notable omissions such as any specific children's rights or a free-standing right to equality. State parties are required to secure all the rights within the Convention to all people within their jurisdiction (Article 1) without discrimination (Article 14) and to ensure that in the event of an interference with a Convention right that there will be an effective remedy (Article 13). Nothing in the Convention can be interpreted as implying any right to destroy the rights in the Convention (Article 17), nor to prevent the state imposing restrictions on the political rights of aliens (Article 16).

The ECHR provides the following substantive rights, prohibitions and freedoms:

- the right to life (Article 2)

- the prohibition of torture and inhuman or degrading treatment and punishment (Article 3)

- the prohibition of forced labour (Article 4)

- the right to liberty and security of the person (Article 5)

- the right to a fair trial (Article 6)

- the prohibition of retrospective criminal penalty (Article 7)

- the right to family and private life (Article 8)

- freedom of conscience (Article 9)

- freedom of expression (Article 10)

- freedom of association (Article 11) and

- the right to marry and found a family (Article 12)

A series of Protocols to the Convention provide additional rights. The UK has ratified the following four Protocols:

- the right to the peaceful enjoyment of personal possessions (Article 1, Protocol 1)

- the right to education (Article 2, Protocol 1)

- the right to free elections (Article 3, Protocol 1)

- abolition of the death penalty (Article 1, Protocol 6)

but has not yet ratified[4] the Protocols which provide for:

- the right not to be imprisoned for failure to fulfil a contractual obligation (Article 1, Protocol 4)

- the right to liberty of movement within the territory of a state (Article 2(1), Protocol 4)

- the freedom to leave any country including her/his own (Article 2(2), Protocol 4)

- the right not to be expelled, collectively or as an individual, from his/her own country (Article 3(1), Protocol 4)

- the right to enter his/her own national state (Article 3(2), Protocol 4)

- the prohibition of the collective expulsion of aliens (Article 4, Protocol 4)

- the right of a lawfully resident alien only to be expelled according to the law (Article 1, Protocol 7)

- the right to criminal appeal (Article 2, Protocol 7)

- the right to compensation on the subsequent quashing of a conviction (Article 3, Protocol 7)

- the right not to be tried or punished for a criminal offence for which the defendant has already been acquitted or convicted (Article 4, Protocol 7)

- the right to equality between spouses in private law (Article 5, Protocol 7).

Although not yet binding on the UK, these latter provisions are not merely of academic interest. The government has recently reviewed its position *vis à vis* those treaty provisions which it has not yet ratified. It has decided that Protocols 4 and 7 will be ratified once an opportunity has arisen to amend certain relevant domestic legislative provisions.

The UK was the first country to ratify the Convention in 1951 and the Article which gave UK citizens the right to complain to the Court of alleged breaches of the Convention was ratified for a temporary period by the Wilson government in 1966. This provision has been renewed ever since, most recently in January 1996 for a further five years.

The ECHR's application to the UK is modified by a reservation entered against Article 2 of the First Protocol.[5] This has been placed on a statutory basis in a Schedule to the Human Rights Act. Article 15 also permits derogation from the Convention during periods of public emergency and the UK has derogated from Article 5(3) in relation to the UK's Prevention of Terrorism legislation.[6]

The Human Rights Act has, for the first time, also placed the derogation from Article 5(3) on a statutory footing and its wording is reproduced in the Schedule to the Act.[7] This derogation, and any later derogations, will be 'designated' under the Act and will cease to have effect after five years unless extended by the Secretary of State by Order for a further five years. Thus, if a derogation is withdrawn, amended or replaced, the Human Rights Act will require amendment. The Secretary of State will therefore be placed under a duty to introduce the necessary amendments and Parliament will have an opportunity to decide whether to approve them.

The supervisory system

There is no systematic scrutiny by the Council of Europe of states' compliance with the Convention, nor any political mechanism to enforce compliance. The Convention is currently enforced by a state party to the Convention, or a victim of an alleged violation, taking a case to the European Court of Human Rights.

Since 1 November 1998, the system for enforcement which then comes into play has fundamentally changed, replacing rules which were judged to have brought unnecessary complexity and length to the conduct of complaints proceedings. There are new arrangements for hearings before a newly constituted Court which will occupy a central position in determining claims under the Convention since the Commission on Human Rights and the Committee of Ministers have both been abolished. The Court's role is to make a final and binding decision as to whether a violation of the Convention has occurred and to consider the question of compensation.

Despite the difficulties and delays attendant on pursuing a complaint under the Convention, many applications have been lodged against the UK and, in a high proportion of cases, the UK has been found in breach. By April 1999, the UK had been judged by the Court to have breached the Convention 52 times.

The growing body of case law has had a profound impact on the UK legal system, prompting a number of significant changes in law and policy concerning, for example, the rights of prisoners[8]; and of detained psychiatric patients[9]; the rights of homosexuals[10]; the fairness of courts martial[11]; the lawful use of phone tapping[12]; the rights of children in care[13] or in education[14]; the freedoms of newspaper editors[15] and journalists[16]; the right to free representation in court proceedings[17] and the physical punishment of children[18].

Limits of the enforcement system

Although the Court of Human Rights has been available to rule in cases such as these, this extra-national enforcement system has proved far from satisfactory for UK citizens. The vast majority of complaints never progress beyond the preliminary stages, the proceedings are protracted and, for those without legal aid, expensive. It can take over five years for an application finally to be determined by the Court. The Council of Europe's recent expansion to include many Central and East European states will put even greater pressure on the capacity of the newly structured Court to deal speedily and proficiently with applications made to it.

For these reasons, the availability of redress from the UK's own courts and tribunals for Convention breaches that will result from the Human Rights Act, will dramatically increase access for UK citizens to their ECHR rights. Nevertheless, it should be recognised that this *judicial* means of ensuring compliance with the Convention usually only comes into play after an alleged breach of the Convention has taken place. While recognising the important deterrent effect which this system may have, it is not a substitute for procedures designed to *prevent* such breaches and a political process which, when government itself is responsible for a breach, enables Parliament to call it to account.

Other Council of Europe treaties

The European Convention on Human Rights is undoubtedly the most important Council of Europe treaty for protecting human rights. However, the Council has agreed a number of other important Conventions to promote human rights standards and issued a number of recommendations, declarations and guidelines. Examples of the latter include the Declaration on Freedom of Expression and Information, and Recommendation No R (87) 8 of the Committee of Ministers to member states regarding conscientious objection to compulsory military service.

The Council's human rights treaties include the European Social Charter, which came into force on 26 February 1965; the European Convention for the Prevention of Torture and Inhuman or Degrading Treatment or Punishment, which came into force on 1 February 1989; and the Framework Convention for the Protection of National Minorities, agreed by the Council of Europe in November 1994 and recently ratified by the UK.

In relation to some of these measures there is a reporting and monitoring procedure, under which states must report on the extent to which they comply with their obligations, but there is (with the exception of the new Protocol to the European Social Chapter) no system for the investigation of individual complaints.

United Nations treaties

The main UN human rights instruments to which the UK is a state party are:

●   The International Covenant on Civil and Political Rights (ICCPR)

●   The International Convention on the Elimination of All Forms of Racial Discrimination (CERD)

●   The Convention on the Elimination of All Forms of Discrimination against Women (CEDAW)

●   The Convention against Torture and Other Cruel, Inhuman or Degrading Treatment or Punishment (CAT)

●   The Convention on the Rights of the Child (CRC)

●   The Covenant on Economic, Social and Cultural Rights

ICCPR

This Convention was adopted in 1966 and entered into force in 1976. It guarantees a wide range of civil and political rights including the rights to life, liberty and security; fair trial; freedom of movement; freedom of thought, conscience and religion; freedom of speech, assembly and association; protection of the family and of children; the right to participate in public life and to vote; and the right to equality and non-discrimination. Each State is required to take whatever legislative or other steps are necessary to give effect to these rights and must ensure that there is an effective remedy in the event of any violation. The UK government ratified the ICCPR on 20 May 1976.

The treaty permits states to derogate from certain of its provisions in times of public emergency. Citing the terrorist campaigns in Northern Ireland, the UK has, since 1988, entered a derogation from Article 9(3), the right to liberty.

The supervisory system[19]

The supervisory body is the Human Rights Committee which is not a UN organ but an independent treaty body. A committee of 18 members, it meets three times a year, twice in Geneva and once in New York. It has two main supervisory functions. The first is to review compulsory reports prepared every five years by each state on the measures taken to implement the provisions of the ICCPR. So far, the UK has had four periodic reports examined by the Human Rights Committee. Its Fourth Report was issued in 1994 and the examination of it took place at the committee's 54th session in Geneva in July 1995.[20]

At that session, the Committee noted that the UK legal system does not fully ensure than an effective remedy is provided for all violations of the rights contained in the Covenant and expressed concern about a wide range of issues including extended periods of detention without charge or access to legal advisers; entry into private property without judicial warrant; conditions in Castlereagh detention centre in Northern Ireland; the strip searching of low security risk prisoners; the high number of suicides in prison; the fact that serious complaints against the police are investigated by the police themselves; the disproportionate use of stop and search procedures against black people; the length of time asylum seekers are detained; limitations on the right to silence; the need for greater effort to change public attitudes towards minorities, and so forth.

The Committee's second main function is the investigation of complaints by individuals of violations of their rights under the ICCPR. Only states which have ratified an optional Protocol to the Convention are subject to the procedure. The UK has not done so.

There is nothing in the ICCPR to make a state party bound by the Committee's decisions in individual cases, including any recommendation for payment of compensation or other redress. Furthermore, the views of the Committee are directed only to the state complained against. There is no doctrine of binding precedent by which the views of the Committee can be applied in other cases or in other states. However, there is now a growing body of jurisprudence developed by the Committee over the years through its consideration of individual complaints. This represents an authoritative source of guidance as to the proper meaning and effect of the Covenant.

CERD

This Convention was adopted in 1965 and entered into force in 1969. It is one of the earliest human rights treaties and is aimed at the comprehensive elimination of racial discrimination. CERD requires states to develop and implement a comprehensive policy to eliminate racial discrimination in all its forms within and outside government and public authorities. States must condemn and outlaw all propaganda and organisations based on theories of racial superiority and ensure that the full range of civil, political, economic, social and cultural rights can be enjoyed by everyone, unhindered by any form of racial discrimination. States must also provide adequate remedies for discrimination and work to eliminate prejudice and to promote tolerance.

On ratification of the Treaty on 7 March 1969, the UK entered a series of interpretative statements and reservations. For example, the UK interprets Article 4 (the prohibition of propaganda and organisations based on theories of racial superiority or the promotion of racial hatred) as requiring legislation only if necessary and with due regard for the rights to freedom of expression, assembly and association.

The supervisory system

CERD provides for an 18-member Committee on the Elimination of Racial Discrimination. This committee normally meets twice a year in Geneva and examines states' periodic reports on their implementation of the Convention. The UK has had thirteen periodic reports examined by CERD. Its 13th report, due in April 1994, was published a year late in April 1995[21] and was examined by the Committee at its 48th session between 26 February and 15 March 1996.[22] The report noted a number of positive steps which had been taken to implement the Convention, such as measures to increase the participation of ethnic minorities in public office and in the police service and the extension of the Race Relations Act (in large part) to Northern Ireland. It expressed a number of areas of concern including the absence of any duty on health, education and social service authorities to promote racial equality.

The Committee's second supervisory function is to investigate individual complaints pursuant to the procedure set out in Article 14 of the Convention. This provision is not automatically binding on states, requiring a special declaration for it to be operative. To date, the UK has declined to make such a declaration. UK citizens are thus not yet able to make individual complaints to the Committee for investigation under this procedure.

CEDAW

This Convention was adopted in 1979 and entered into force in 1981. The Convention outlaws discrimination against women in all its forms and requires states to develop a comprehensive policy in this regard within and outside government and public authorities. The UK ratified CEDAW on 7 April 1986.

The Convention requires measures to modify social and cultural patterns of discrimination and prejudice; measures to suppress traffic in women and sexual exploitation; equality in access to, and participation in, political and public life; equal rights in the fields of nationality, education and training, employment and conditions of work, health care, economic and social life, freedom of movement, marriage and family relations and in legal matters; and special protection for rural women.

This Convention suffers more than others from the large number of reservations entered by states, including the UK. However, the UK has decided to withdraw those reservations considered no longer necessary. One reservation still in force provides that the guarantees of equal treatment in relation to freedom of movement are subject to 'such UK immigration legislation as may be deemed necessary from time to time for anyone without the right to enter and remain in the UK'.

The supervisory system

The supervisory body provided for in CEDAW is a Committee on the Elimination of Discrimination against Women composed of twenty three experts. This committee, which used to be based in Vienna, was recently moved to New York. The Convention itself provides that the committee should normally meet for only two weeks a year, but this has since been extended to take account of the committee's huge backlog of work.

However, this committee is the only treaty body which is not serviced by the UN Centre for Human Rights in Geneva and which holds none of its meetings there. As a result of this and other factors it has been isolated and an acute lack of resources and exclusion from the treaty-monitoring system have weakened its effectiveness.

The committee monitors the implementation of the Convention by reviewing the periodic reports of states parties. Under Article 18, states parties must report within one year of the treaty coming into force and thereafter every four years. There is no individual complaints procedure under this Convention, though its possible introduction is under discussion.

The UK submitted its initial report in 1987 and this was considered by the committee in 1990. Its second periodic report was submitted in 1991 and examined in 1993.[23] The third report was published in July 1995.

CAT

This Convention was adopted in 1984 and entered into force in 1987. It outlaws torture in any circumstances and requires states to make such activity a criminal offence and to establish universal jurisdiction over alleged torturers. No one may be extradited or sent back to any country where they may face torture. States must take steps to prosecute or extradite alleged torturers and must introduce proper systems for lodging complaints. The CAT also deals with measures for prevention and protection, including keeping interrogation techniques under review and ensuring proper education and training for law enforcement officials. The UK ratified the CAT on 8 December 1988 and made no reservations to it.

The supervisory system

CAT provides for the establishment of a ten member supervisory Committee against Torture. Members meet twice a year in Geneva. The committee examines reports submitted by states parties every four years. The UK's initial report on implementation was considered in 1991 and it has since submitted two periodic reports. In its most recent report on the UK, in 1998, the Committee welcomed the introduction of the Human Rights Act, and the 'Peace Process' in Northern Ireland, but expressed concern *inter alia* about the number of deaths in police custody and the 'apparent failure of the State party to provide an effective investigative mechanism to deal with allegations of police and prison authorities' abuse'. It was also concerned about the use of prisons to house refugee claimants, the continued use of Castlereagh detention centre and the use in Northern Ireland of plastic bullets as a means of riot control.[24] Given the current political debate on some of these issues, such as the question of an independent mechanism to investigate complaints against the police, it is striking that the recommendations of this international body are not well known and rarely enter the debate.

There is an individual complaints procedure but this requires a declaration of acceptance and the UK has not yet submitted such a declaration. There is also a unique procedure under Article 20 of the CAT by which the committee can investigate allegations of the systematic practice of torture in a state party. No prior acceptance of this procedure is required, although states parties can decide to opt out of it at the time of ratification. The UK did not opt out. In therefore remains subject to this procedure if sufficiently credible and grave allegations of the systematic practice of torture in the UK were ever to be made to the Committee.

CRC

This Convention was adopted in 1989 and entered into force in 1990. The treaty has attracted more ratifications, at a faster rate, than any other human rights treaty and is already rapidly approaching universal ratification by all UN member states.

The Convention is a comprehensive charter of the human rights of children covering civil, political, economic, social and cultural rights including life, liberty and physical security; exploitation and various forms of abuse; identity and nationality; contacts with parents, adoption and other forms of care; freedom of expression, thought, conscience and religion; freedom of assembly and association; health and disability; an adequate standard of living and social benefits; education; minority rights; recruitment into the armed forces; and the criminal justice system. The best interests of the child are to be the primary consideration and children have the right to express their own views on matters affecting them.

When the UK ratified the Convention on 16 December 1991 it made a number of declarations and reservations. These included, for example, a general reservation to ensure that the UK can continue to apply any immigration and citizenship legislation it deems necessary; and that children may be held in custody with adults if there is a lack of suitable separate accommodation or it is considered beneficial to do so.

The supervisory system

A 10-member Committee on the Rights of the Child meets for three sessions a year in Geneva. The main supervisory task of the committee is the review of periodic reports on implementation. The UK's initial report was examined in January 1995[25] and resulted in a highly critical report from the Committee. The next report is in preparation for submission in 1999. There is no individual complaints procedure under this Convention.

ICESCR

This Covenant was adopted in 1966 and entered into force in 1976. Its provisions include the right to work and conditions at work, the right to join trade unions, to protection for the family and for pregnant women, the exploitation of children, adequate standard of living, compulsory primary education, standards of health, and the right to participate in cultural life.

The Covenant is supervised by the UN's Economic and Social Council to which states submit periodic reports. On reviewing the UK's last report in 1997, in addition to recommending that the UK introduce a system of human rights impact statements (*above*), the Committee expressed concern about, *inter alia*, unacceptable levels of poverty, the widening gap between rich and poor, the failure to incorporate the right to strike into domestic law, the extent of homelessness, the religious segregation of education in Northern Ireland, and the number of children permanently excluded from school.[26]

Impact of the UN treaties in the UK

Several factors weaken the impact of the UN treaties on this country. The UK's failure to date to ratify the right to individual petition, where this is available, means that no case law under the respective treaty has developed on our domestic law or its remedies.

The UN Committees responsible for monitoring implementation have each insisted that, in the absence of the right to individual petition, treaties cannot be effectively implemented. The Committee on the Elimination of Racial Discrimination, for example, has concluded in relation to the UK that:

> The legal framework prohibiting racial discrimination is further weakened by the non-incorporation of the Convention into domestic legislation, the absence of a bill of rights espousing the principle of equality before the law and non-discrimination and the lack of recourse of individuals to petition an international body such as the Committee.[27]

The Committee on the Convention Against Torture has come to a similar conclusion. It has stated that:

> The Committee regrets that invocation of the Convention by individuals is not possible since the UK has not declared in favour of Article 22 of the Convention. This appears unusual

given that the UK has acceded to the jurisdiction of the European Commission of Human Rights.[28]

Past UK governments have chosen to ignore UN recommendations when it has suited them, causing one former UK member of the UN Human Rights Committee to lament such indifference:

> It is a sad thing when one now hears it announced here in the United Kingdom that there is no intention to act on any of the Committee's recommendations, because 'they (the UN Committee) do not understand our culture'. What is this culture, that cannot be understood by American, French, German and Italian members of the Committee, not to mention Commonwealth Supreme Court Justices?[29]

In addition, the UN's endemic funding problems have limited the effectiveness of the monitoring bodies, delaying their procedures, restricting the resources available to them to manage the work of the Committees and the dissemination of their findings and recommendations.[30]

However, as we argued in relation to the ECHR, even if the system for calling the UK to account at the international level were effective it would not replace the need for effective national systems to prevent law and practices breaching international standards.

The European Union

The European Union plays an increasingly significant role in promoting and protecting human rights standards – most recently in relation to data protection (privacy) but particularly in relation to rights of full and equal participation by citizens of member states in the Union's labour market. Freedom of movement is a right guaranteed under EC law and standards of equality between women and men in employment and social security have, for example, been set by the European Union's Court of Justice. The Amsterdam Treaty has extended the law making powers of the European Community to include measures designed to combat discrimination on far wider grounds: race, sexual orientation, disability and religion.

The Treaty on Economic Union (TEU), or the Maastricht Treaty, also made overt reference, in Article F2, to the fact that the Union will respect the fundamental rights guaranteed by the ECHR. The more recent Amsterdam Treaty has given further recognition to the ECHR as a foundation of Community Law. It is hard to predict what the long term impact of this change will be but it will undoubtedly highlight the importance for the EU institutions and member states of ensuring that their policies and laws comply with the Convention.

As significant, EU measures can have a negative effect on human rights, for instance those on immigration and asylum and, potentially, its pan-European measures on policing. Prior to agreement on such measures, the UK should satisfy itself that implementing the measures will not breach its international human rights undertakings.

Norms and guidelines

In addition to those standards found in legally-binding international treaties, there is a broad range of other international norms and standards which are designed to influence state practice in the protection of individual human rights. Norms and guidelines have been adopted by the United Nations, for example, in relation to the protection of minority groups and to the prohibition of religious intolerance and of violence against women. Non-binding recommendations, rules and standards have also been adopted by the Council of Europe dealing with issues as diverse as prison conditions, the use of minority languages and the professional ethics of the police.

The UK has played its full part in the drafting and adoption of these non-treaty human rights instruments. Although such declarations and guidelines are not legally binding (and therefore require no formal act of recognition or acceptance by states), they carry moral and political weight. They represent basic minimum standards agreed upon by the international community collectively, often by consensus. States are expected to strive to adhere to them and respect them in their own legislation, policies and practices.

For some UN standards there is even a very rudimentary form of international monitoring. Periodic questionnaires are sent to all UN member states requesting them to report on implementation. The answers are then compiled and considered by a UN body such as its Commission on Criminal Justice and Crime Prevention. This system of monitoring is far from perfect, being entirely voluntary and dependent on states replying to lengthy questionnaires. Nevertheless, it does serve to remind states of the existence of these non-binding standards and of their importance for human rights protection.

Conclusion

The UK has ratified a number of Conventions, binding under international law, which contain a wealth of detailed provisions and together constitute a comprehensive body of human rights standards. With the exception of the ECHR, these international treaties have had limited domestic impact on the conduct of public or private bodies and on the rights and obligations of individual citizens, despite the fact that the international committees supervising the UK's treaty obligations have pointed to a number of areas of concern about law and practice in Britain and Northern Ireland .

The Human Rights Act will increase the significance and accessibility to UK citizens and organisations of the provisions of the ECHR, not only by providing immediate remedies in the UK courts but by leading to preventative measures. This will build on the influence already seen to result from the right of individual petition applicable in the UK since 1966.

For the wider international standards to be effective in the UK there need, first, to be procedures in Whitehall and Parliament which check whether proposed legislation and policies comply with these standards. In order to ensure that the standards are adopted more widely in the public and private sector, the terms of these Conventions need to be widely known.

Endnotes

1. An Article not incorporated into the Human Rights Act.
2. *Concluding observations of the Committee on Economic, Social and Cultural Rights, United Kingdom of Great Britain and Northern Ireland* 4 December 1997, E/C.12/1/Add.19.
3. This principle, however, should have no relevance when the provisions of the Human Rights Act are interpreted within the UK's domestic courts.

4. See Written Answer 201 on 4 March 1999 in which the government stated that it will ratify the 4th and 7th protocols when it has been able to amend certain domestic legislative provisions.

5. The reservation states:

    '... in view of certain provisions of the Education Act in the UK the principles affirmed in the second sentence of Article 2 is accepted by the UK only so far as is compatible with the provisions of efficient instruction and training, and the avoidance of unreasonable public expenditure.'

6. Prevention of Terrorism (Temporary Provisions) Act 1984 s.2; Prevention of Terrorism (Supplemental Temporary Provisions) Order 1984 Article 9; and Prevention of Terrorism (Supplemental Temporary Provisions) (Northern Ireland) Order 1984.

7. Schedule 3, Part I, Human Rights Act 1998.

8. Silver and others -v- United Kingdom [1983] 3 EHRR 475; Thynne, Wilson and Gunnell -v- United Kingdom [1990] 13 EHRR 666.

9. X -v- United Kingdom [1981] 4 EHRR 188

10. Dudgeon -v- United Kingdom [1982] 4 EHRR 149

11. Findlay -v- United Kingdom [1997] 24 EHRR 221

12. Malone -v- United Kingdom [1984] 7 EHRR 14

13. O, H, W, B, R -v- United Kingdom [1987] 10 EHRR 82

14. Campbell -v- Cosans [1982] 4 EHRR 293

15. *Sunday Times* -v- United Kingdom [1979] 2 EHRR 245

16. Goodwin -v- United Kingdom [1996] 22 EHRR 123

17. Boner -v- United Kingdom [1995] 19 EHRR 246

18. A -v- United Kingdom [1998] Z FLR 959; 100/1997/884/1096

19. For a review of the work and impact of the Committee, see Higgins R 'Opinion: Ten years on the UN Human Rights Committee: some thoughts upon parting' [1996] 6 EHRLR 570-582

20. The UK's Fourth Report is contained in UN Document CCPR/C/95/Add.3. The summary records of the review are to be found in UN Documents CCPR/C/SR.1432 to 1434 and the Committee's concluding Comments in UN Document CCPR/C/79/Add.55.

21. CERD/C/263/Add.7 & CERD/C/263/Add.7 Part II.

22. CERD/C/SR.1139, 1140 & 1141.

23. The first report was contained in UN Document CEDAW/C/5/Add.

52 and Amends. 1-4. It was examined by the Committee in 1990. For the summary records see UN Documents CEDAW/C/SR. 155, 156, 159 and 160. The second report was contained in UN Document CEDAW/C/UK/2 and Amend 1. For its examination in 1993 see UN Document CEDAW/C/SR.223.

24. UN Press Release *Committee against Torture issues conclusions and recommendations on reports of the United Kingdom and Hungary* 19 November 1998 HR/CAT/98/42

25. The report is contained in UN Document CRC/C/11/Add.1. The summary records of the Committee's examination are to be found in CRC/C/SR.204-206 and its Concluding Observations in UN Document CRC/C/15/Add.34.

26. *Concluding observations of the Committee on Economic, Social and Cultural Rights* 4 December 1997, E/C.12/1/Add.19.

27. *Concluding observations of the Committee on the Elimination of Racial Discrimination, 48h session* 26 February-15 March 1996.

28. CAT/C/SR. 234 and 235.

29. Higgins R, *op cit* p576.

30. Higgins R, *op cit* p581.

3. Human rights scrutiny in Whitehall and Westminster

We saw in Chapter 2 that a body of international human rights standards now apply to the United Kingdom. These are not static but develop as new agreements are made and existing ones interpreted. The UK's compliance is monitored, and in the case of the ECHR enforced, at the international level. However, to rely on that system would be to depend on procedures which are reactive, patchy, and largely ineffectual. Supervision by UN Committee gathers relatively limited information, occurs only periodically and the Committee can merely express its views in the hope that these will be heeded. Even where well respected by governments, the international arrangements for external oversight cannot replace effective domestic procedures to ensure that law, policy and practice comply with the international standards.

Current procedures for such scrutiny, both in Whitehall and in Westminster, are modest and marginal to the business of the executive and legislature. It is accepted by the government that they must now be developed to meet the demands both of the Human Rights Act and our wider international obligations.

This Chapter details where changes are needed and why. After describing what we mean by 'scrutiny' we consider how government proposals for primary and secondary legislation, and for policy, are currently tested for their compatibility with international human rights standards. We pinpoint the limitations of the present system which the new procedures must avoid if they are to be more effective.

Scrutiny defined

What does it mean for the government or Parliament to scrutinise policy or legislative proposals for compliance with international human rights standards? When human rights impact statements are produced, what issues should they address?

An established body of written instruments and caselaw in the human rights field can now be applied to any proposal in order to test whether or not it is likely to conflict with international legal standards. The ECHR and the decisions made under this Convention form one of the most substantial and developed sources of such law. Together they constitute a jurisprudence which will shortly become directly enforceable in the UK courts. Our judges are expressly required to take this into account when deciding cases under the Human Rights Act.

As they do so, we can expect our courts to regard the standards set in Strasbourg as minimum rather than maximum ones. The doctrine of the 'margin of appreciation', by which the European Court of Human Rights has justified its non-interference in some cases, permitting State Parties to determine for themselves how Convention rights will be respected in their jurisdiction, is unlikely to apply when UK judges are called upon to interpret the rights now found in the Human Rights Act.

Proposals from government for new policies or for law may, inadvertently or deliberately, restrict the rights in the ECHR or the rights found in UN treaties such as the ICCPR. Not all human rights are of the same order and the scrutiny process differs according to the nature of the right which is at issue. Thus, for instance, the process of scrutiny not only has to establish whether a right has been infringed but, in many cases, whether the circumstances justified that restriction. In some cases, the issue is not whether a right has been infringed by the state but whether it has failed to take positive steps to protect that right.

There are essentially three kinds of rights in the ECHR and in the other international human rights instruments:

- *Absolute rights:* such as the right to life, freedom from torture and protection from retrospective penalties, from which governments are not allowed to derogate (seek exemption) even in times of emergency. (The ECHR occasionally allows specific exemptions from such rights, such as deaths resulting from necessary force in self defence).

- *Rights with defined exemptions:* such as the right to liberty, where the basic entitlement can be disapplied with reference to a list of specific, exempted situations or categories of person (such as the lawful detention of a person after conviction by a court).

- *Qualified rights:* such as the right to private and family life, which must be interpreted with reference to several general considerations including the need to protect the rights of others or the need to prevent crime or to protect national security. Any attempt to restrict qualified rights on these grounds must be proportional to that need and 'necessary in a democratic society'.

Absolute rights

The process of scrutiny must take account of these distinctions. Absolute rights do not have to be balanced against other competing rights. The task for scrutiny is thus usually only to establish if the act or omission could result in a breach of the right. Home Office policy approving, for example, the use of CS spray by police officers or permitting the use, within the prison service, of physical restraint would thus need to be scrutinised to establish whether these could sanction behaviour which could improperly threaten life or cause inhuman or degrading treatment.

Rights with defined exemptions

Scrutinising proposals for their effect on rights with defined exemptions, however, requires an interpretation of the circumstances in which those rights may be restricted. They do not, however, involve any balancing of interests or rights. The question for scrutiny is, first, whether the right is likely to be restricted and, if so, whether the circumstances used to justify it fall within those specified in the Convention. Thus proposals providing for the detention of asylum seekers would need, under Article 5 of the ECHR, to be examined against the specific grounds in Article 5 under which detention is permitted, such as 'the lawful arrest or detention of a person to prevent his effecting an unauthorised entry into the country or of a person against whom action is being taken with a view to deportation or extradition'.

Qualified rights

To identify whether or not qualified rights are restricted, there is an established three stage test for determining whether the restrictions are acceptable.[1] Each of the three elements of this test must be fulfilled for any restriction to be judged lawful. Scrutiny here involves a balancing exercise which necessitates a consideration of wider factors:

● Is the restriction prescribed by law? In other words, can ordinary citizens discover that the restriction exists and, if so, is the law formulated clearly enough for citizens to regulate their conduct?

- Does it comply with the recognised aims found in the ECHR which justify some restriction or qualification of the right or freedom? In other words, does the restriction aim, for instance, to protect the rights of others, or to prevent public disorder or crime?

- Lastly, is the restriction necessary in a democratic society? A state must be able to show that the restriction both fulfils a pressing social need and is 'proportionate' to the aim of responding to that need. It must demonstrate that the restriction arises from genuine concerns and does not amount to an overreaction.

Given the nature of these questions and the manner in which human rights law is drafted and interpreted, there can be some uncertainty associated with the scrutiny process where rights are limited in this way. It will demand an approach which addresses moral and social questions as well as legal and political ones.

Identifying whether a proposal might infringe or restrict a right is a relatively straightforward operation, involving the application of relevant principles and caselaw to the wording of draft legislation or administrative policy. However, weighing up the substantive justification for any intended restriction against the harm resulting to human rights is far more uncertain and contentious. With the ECHR this is particularly so given the difficulties of accurately predicting how the European Court of Human Rights, and soon our domestic courts, would determine the question if required to rule upon it.

Effective scrutiny should therefore require an assessment of information and opinions drawn from a range of sources, not exclusively legal ones. It should include the gathering of legal advice offered in the light of current jurisprudence; the views of those who may be affected by the proposal (positively and negatively) and social data relevant to the rights in question and the ways in which proposals may restrict them. Only then will it be possible to evaluate whether or not the restriction is genuinely needed and is proportionate to the specific aim being pursued. Current procedures for scrutiny in Whitehall and in Westminster do not, however, meet that test.

Scrutiny in Whitehall

A proposal for new policy or legislation may come from a number of sources: a party's political programme; pressure from NGOs; difficulties in implementing existing law which require urgent changes; or recommendations from the Law Commission, a Royal Commission or a Departmental Committee. Unforeseen events can force urgent changes on to the government's agenda. The banning of handguns following the Dunblane Inquiry report or the anti-terrorist legislation in the wake of the Omagh bombing in 1998 are examples. Court decisions, including those of the European Court of Human Rights, may create a need to amend legislation or introduce some fresh measure. A Declaration of Incompatibility under s.4 of the Human Rights Act, for example, is likely to result in a review of legislation, if not a proposal to amend it. Sometimes, developments in international relations prompt legislative reform. The government might agree to ratify an international treaty or protocol which requires a change in the law before it can be fully implemented.

Administrative procedures govern the way in which a proposal is developed into a viable and approved policy and the preparation of any draft legislation needed to implement it. Those procedures include Cabinet Office guidance to officials, and to Ministers, on the question of compatibility with the ECHR.

'Strasbourg-proofing'

Given the enforceability of the ECHR at Strasbourg, it is this Convention which has always had greatest prominence in Whitehall. The mechanism by which policy and proposed legislation has been assessed for conformity to the ECHR is known as 'Strasbourg-proofing'. It resulted from two Cabinet Office circulars issued to government departments in July 1987 in recognition of a 'consistently high level of applications and decisions [before the Strasbourg human rights institutions] which concern the UK'.[2] The procedure advocated in these circulars is reiterated in the 1996 Cabinet Office *Guide to Legislative Procedures*.

The first of the circulars, *Reducing the Risk of Legal Challenge*, specifically refers to the ECHR in the course of general guidance on the conditions that Departments need to be aware of in order to minimise the risk of legal challenge when preparing legislative proposals. As part of these concerns, it addresses procedures to reduce a successful challenge in Strasbourg pointing out that 'questions on it [the Convention] can sometimes arise in most of the areas of law administered by departments'. The full text of the circular is reproduced in the Appendix (p103).

The *Guide to Legislative Procedures*, drawing on this circular, says:

> It should be standard practice when preparing a policy initiative for officials in individual departments, in consultation with their legal advisers, to consider the effect of existing (or expected) ECHR jurisprudence on any proposed legislative or administrative measure... If departments are in any doubt about the likely implications of the Convention in connection with any particular measure, they should seek ad hoc guidance from the Foreign and Commonwealth Office.[3]

The Guide states that any memoranda submitted to a Cabinet committee, or accompanying a Bill submitted to Legislation Committee, should include an assessment of the impact, if any, of the ECHR on the action proposed. The government intends to strengthen this procedure by requiring officials to make an assessment of compliance with the ECHR at an earlier stage when a Minister seeks approval for the policy to which an Act will later give effect.

The Cabinet Office's *Questions of Procedure for Ministers* reinforces the message, requiring Ministers when putting proposals to Cabinet or to a Ministerial Committee to cover, where possible, the impact of the ECHR.[4] The notes, however, neither specify how this should be undertaken nor how its results should be presented. Since it is a memorandum to Cabinet, the ECHR assessment is not in the normal course of events made public.

David Kinley, a legal expert on scrutiny procedures, has commented on this approach:

> The informality of this process (if it can be called such), and the scope for its inconsistent exercise throughout the departments are factors that have hardly aided its

effectiveness. Indeed, there is irony in the fact that the same year in which these Cabinet circulars were published also marked a sharp increase in the rate at which the European Court has found against the United Kingdom. Whereas 13 violations can be attributed to the eleven-year period 1975-1986, judgements against the United Kingdom were handed down by the court on 27 occasions in the nine years between 1987 and 1996. In light of these statistics, one might note with regret, that the fact that the second edition (published in 1994) of the 'Judge over your shoulder' Memorandum failed to mention the ECHR at all may make little difference as the Memorandum's original exhortation to ensure compliance appears to have had minimal effect.[5]

Expertise

FCO officials make an important contribution to the 'Strasbourg-proofing' process if departmental lawyers are concerned that proposals may be in breach of the ECHR. Its lawyers are acknowledged to be leading authorities on international human rights standards and work alongside, but are not part of, the Human Rights Policy Department within the FCO. The FCO has ultimate responsibility in the UK for the reporting process under the UN international human rights treaties and has a responsibility to ensure that the UK fulfils its international obligations.

Although FCO lawyers are experts in the field of human rights, government relies on a hierarchy of legal advice. If the proposal for legislation or policy under examination is significant enough it will also be reviewed by the Attorney General and Solicitor General. Where there is serious concern about the conformity of a particular measure with the ECHR, advice from outside Counsel may also be sought.

Wider international standards

What of Whitehall's scrutiny of policy for its conformity to Conventions other than the ECHR? There is evidence that government departments may consider the relevance of some of these treaties when finalising proposals for new legislation. For example, the lead department on the

UN Convention on the Rights of the Child, the Department of Health, conducts a full internal review, including legal advice as necessary, in respect of legislative proposals, to ensure conformity with the CRC.[6] However, it is less clear that other departments undertake any such exercise before similarly introducing legislative or policy proposals. Little priority appears to be given towards ensuring compliance with the broad range of less well known international standards to which the UK is a party.

'Strasbourg-proofing': lessons from past practice

The government intends to replace the Strasbourg proofing guidance with an updated version fitted to the new demands of the Human Rights Act. In our view, the need for reform is highlighted by the limitations of the existing procedure:

● It is predominantly concerned with avoiding adverse findings against the UK and is thus an exercise in risk management. It does not suggest how departments might seek to move beyond the limited objective of compliance towards the implementation of good practice.

● The current guidance does not seek to ensure compliance with the UK's wider international obligations, such as the ICCPR.

● The procedure does not assist *Parliament* to identify where draft legislation might impose restrictions on Convention rights in breach of its provisions. Section 19 of the Human Rights Act, requiring Ministers to make a statement to Parliament, on the compatibility of each Bill with the Convention, will specifically address this problem but may not be sufficient, for reasons we give below.

● The guidance was written in the context of potential enforcement of a small number of cases, over a lengthy timescale, by the European Court of Human Rights, rather than immediate enforcement by UK Courts under the Human Rights Act.

As a result of these factors, knowledge of the ECHR and the priority given to its requirements was far from consistent throughout Whitehall. To be effective in conveying the need for a fresh start and a rigorous approach to scrutiny the new guidance will need to move beyond a narrow risk management approach, and will need to involve Parliament as a check on the executive.

Mainstreaming[7] and PAFT

The assessment of new policy and law for its possible impact on the rights of citizens has been most developed in Northern Ireland with the introduction of the PAFT (Policy Appraisal and Fair Treatment) guidelines. PAFT involves more than scrutiny for compliance with a set of legal principles (broadly those establishing equal treatment and anti-discrimination rights) since the impact of proposals on social groups must also be considered.

The Policy Appraisal and Fair Treatment Guidelines, issued to Northern Ireland Office (NIO) Departments and the public sector in 1993 and operational from 1 January 1994, have, at least on paper, required an unprecedented degree of equality proofing prior to the implementation of new policy or introduction of new services. We summarise the key sections of the PAFT guidance in the box below. It is unusual for the prominence which it accords to explicit human rights principles; for the action check list to be used in the appraisal process; for the requirement for departments to report regularly to the Secretary of State and for the publication of all such departmental reports in an annual NIO report[8] – a unique contribution to accountability in this field.

Policy Appraisal and Fair Treatment Guidelines: Key points

Promotion of positive and proactive approach to equality and equity in policy and services

A fair treatment dimension in all policy-making and when new service provision is considered, from outset of process not just at its end

Measures to avoid discrimination on grounds of religion, political belief, gender, marital status, having or not having a dependant, ethnicity, disability, age or sexual orientation

Implementation through a defined appraisal process, by monitoring and an annual reporting system

---

The guidance is wide in its scope and appears to be relatively demanding of those framing policy. Part of paragraph 3 of the Circular reads:

> The prevention of direct discrimination alone is not enough to promote equality of opportunity and fair treatment. This requires a more positive approach to take whatever measures may be necessary in practice in order to identify and remove any unjustified factors which may result in unequal treatment.

Paragraph 6 reads:

> This guidance is designed to help Departments and Agencies to build in considerations of fair treatment from the outset, in their preparation of policy proposals, including legislation, other initiatives and strategic plans for the implementation of policy and the delivery of services.

Paragraph 19 commences with the following guidance:

> When policy options and legislative proposals are put forward for consideration by Ministers, the submission should always confirm that the implications of PAFT have been taken into account; where a PAFT appraisal has been carried out the submission should set out any conclusions of the appraisal which indicate that adoption of any particular option would have an adverse differential effect...

Annex 1 to the guidelines lists key measures 'to protect human rights and to prevent discrimination'. These do not just include the domestic laws to combat political and religious discrimination, sectarian hatred and bias in public administration. Also covered are Northern Ireland's legislation on sex discrimination and on police misconduct, the ECHR and the many United Nations Conventions protecting human rights.

PAFT replaced

PAFT has now been implemented for a number of years – enough time for an assessment of its usefulness and potential. The guidance and process were welcomed by organisations within Northern Ireland[9] but doubts about its effective implementation led to calls for the guidance to be placed on a statutory footing to give it much-needed status[10] and establish its priority in relation to other policies of government[11]. When the Standing Advisory Commission on Human Rights (SACHR) reviewed Fair Employment legislation in force in Northern Ireland[12] it concluded that implementation of the policy to date had 'fallen far short of what might reasonably have been expected in an area of such importance'. A more systematic approach was required and the aim of the procedure strengthened.

SACHR recommended that the objectives and requirements of PAFT should be given legislative form and introduced in a clear statutory framework. The duty on government at the heart of the policy should be defined in law; a list of the bodies to which it applied should be scheduled in regulations and a Code of Practice should give clear directions as to how proposals for policy or service delivery should be appraised. SACHR recommended that each new proposal for legislation should be accompanied by an assessment of its impact for equality.

In the subsequent White Paper *Partnership for Equality*[13] the government argued:

> PAFT is about a process of appraisal. It can highlight factors which might not otherwise have been taken into account in decision making, but these can only inform, not determine, the final decision. This is also the case with appraisals for which there is statutory requirement, such as environmental impact assessments. As an administrative mechanism, the PAFT process is inevitably limited. It is unrealistic to expect it to carry the legal and constitutional weight which some have claimed for it.[14]

Despite these observations, the government decided that PAFT should be superseded by a more robust duty defined within a statutory framework and monitored by a new combined statutory Equality

Commission. That approach was established by the Northern Ireland Act 1998 which also established the Human Rights Commission[15]. Under the Act, each public authority will be expected to adopt a statutory equality scheme setting out how it proposes to have regard to promote equality.

Equality-proofing in Britain

Appraisal of policy for its equality implications elsewhere in the UK can hardly be compared even with the present Northern Ireland system. So far, it has not moved far beyond 'equality proofing' in relation to gender and race in accordance with less rigorous guidance first issued to Whitehall in 1990 and revised in 1996. Fresh guidance was issued jointly by the Cabinet Office, Home Office and the DfEE in November 1998. *Policy Appraisal for Equal Treatment*, requires impact assessments to be made on grounds of race, gender, disability and age, and is described in more detail in Chapter 4. Although the guidance refers to the need to ensure compliance with international standards on discrimination, no mention is made in the guidance of the parallel Strasbourg-proofing process.

Scrutiny in Westminster: primary legislation[16]

The White Paper, *Rights Brought Home*, signalled the possibility that Parliament might establish a Human Rights Committee to give human rights a higher profile in Westminster. The Committee is expected to be established during 1999 and begin work in the Autumn. Our analysis of the current situation shows this to be very necessary – not least to undertake scrutiny of legislation.

Parliament's present approach to examining proposed legislation for its conformity to human rights standards is characterised by a lack of focus and effective organisation. This reflects the absence of specialised procedures – and any Select Committee with responsibility in this area.

MPs and peers have had to rely on Parliament's ordinary procedures and practices. Determining the human rights compatibility of proposed legislation has in the past been regarded as peripheral. It has not attracted much priority as a constitutional issue within the overall system of legislative scrutiny.

Thus, although Hansard reports have contained references to argument in both Houses of Parliament on the human rights dimension of draft legislation, such consideration was often *ad hoc*, unsystematic and largely reliant on the personal interest and expertise of Opposition members in both Houses. Scrutiny has often amounted to little more than an MP or peer on the Opposition benches (and in the Lords from the Cross benches) asserting that a particular clause or part of a clause is not compatible with a particular human rights principle, followed by the responsible government Minister stating, without more explanation, that indeed it is. Prior to the Human Rights Act, there has been no parliamentary procedure to assess the conformity of Bills, delegated legislation or policy with the UK's human rights obligations.

Parliamentary procedures offer a range of options for the detailed consideration of legislation or policy. Standing Committees, and very occasionally Special Standing Committees, are formed to give detailed consideration to specific Bills. Departmental Select Committees, which conduct inquiries into specific aspects of that department's work or policy, do not traditionally play any role in relation to draft legislation. Nor do they normally express a view on the compatibility of legislation or policy with international human rights standards. They are not prevented from doing so, however, and, on rare occasions, they do.[17]

The need for careful, thorough and robust scrutiny by Parliament cannot be overstated. Ministers, in their enthusiasm for the measures they propose, may be more inclined to reject advice that a particular measure may breach the Convention than Parliament would be willing to do. Scrutiny by both Houses should prevent, in some instances, the passing of laws which may violate the UK's international obligations. It also will improve the quality of legislation by making its purpose and effect clearer. As we show in the following chapter, scrutiny procedures do not have to be excessively onerous or bureaucratic; nor will they impede the passage of legislation unduly.

With UK courts about to assume a new role in enforcing the ECHR, effective scrutiny will become all the more necessary if judges are to discover the intentions of Parliament *vis a vis* the Convention. Unclear or obtuse drafting of legislation is bound to lead to costly and disruptive court challenges: pre-legislative scrutiny is likely to save the government time, rather than delay its programme unnecessarily. Our research revealed several examples of legislation, successfully challenged under the ECHR in Strasbourg, which would have benefited from closer scrutiny and clarification during its passage through Parliament.[18]

In designing the new system of Parliamentary scrutiny, certain lessons can be learnt by examining some of the debates on primary legislation in previous Parliaments where human rights issues have been raised. These may be summarised as follows:

Insufficient expertise

Members, particularly of the House of Commons, have been unable to deploy sufficient expertise on international human rights law and the UK's obligations. They have had no means of obtaining clear legal advice, apart from that supplied to them by lobbyists and pressure groups.[19] The government, on the other hand, has had ready access to professional advice.

Inadequate consideration

The time allocated to considering proposed legislation has sometimes limited opportunities for careful deliberation on the risk of human rights being restricted. This is so especially where the need for urgent legislation has resulted in drastically curtailed debate, aided by the use of a guillotine motion. A full examination of its compatibility with human rights standards is then not possible. With some legislation, such haste can be shown to have resulted in consequences that could have been easily predicted and avoided had more time been permitted.[20]

Limited government accountability

Government is able to influence much of what goes on in Parliament. When such power has been combined with an unsystematic approach to evaluating the human rights questions raised by proposed legislation, Ministers have found it relatively easy to evade even soundly argued challenges that their proposals will fail to conform with international law. The absence of formal procedures or parliamentary institutions with a mandate to raise human rights issues has meant that Ministers have often not needed to answer the detailed points made in debate or give their reasons for rejecting them save in broad terms.[21]

The role of opposition parties

The absence of any all-party focus for scrutiny has ensured that the task of raising human rights implications has fallen to opposition parties. This has created the impression that human rights questions are party political rather than the responsibility of the whole House. It has also meant that concern about how their position will be represented to voters by Ministers or the press has sometimes stifled criticism when this was badly needed during the consideration of draft legislation.[22]

Subordinate legislation[23]

Draft subordinate legislation also requires scrutiny. Incorporation of the ECHR will empower the courts to declare such legislation invalid if it is judged to breach the Convention. Such legislation constitutes a major source of law and grows year by year. Indeed, the quantity, scope and increasing complexity of these measures create enormous pressures for those presently responsible for scrutiny against non-human rights criteria.

The number of instruments subject to a Parliamentary procedure rose by 50 per cent in the 15 years until 1996, from 1000 to around 1500 per year with instruments subject only to the negative resolution procedure nearly doubling from around 700 in the early 1980s to over 1300 in 1994-95. A report from the House of Commons Procedure Committee also identified a change in the content of the legislation, noting that it included policy as well as points of detailed regulation, thus leading to longer and more complex instruments.[24]

Research shows that subordinate legislation is as likely to breach international human rights law as primary legislation. Kinley has shown that of the 22 (out of 28)[25] ECHR violations by the UK between 1975 and 1991, eight involved some form of subordinate legislation.

The Joint Committee on Statutory Instruments considers all statutory instruments which are presented to Parliament to check whether they comply with a specified set of criteria. It does not consider the merits of the instrument; only whether, for instance, its scope ranges beyond that envisaged by the original act, and whether there are any public revenue implications, reporting any concerns it may have to Parliament. The criteria specified in its terms of reference do *not* include any explicit reference to compatibility with the UK's international human rights obligations.

European Community legislation

On the UK's accession to the European Community the then government assured Parliament that special arrangements would be devised under which both Houses would be consulted on draft Community legislation before crucial decisions were taken in Brussels.[26] On 30 October 1980 a resolution was passed by the House of Commons that the government would not agree to a European proposal whilst either House maintained its 'Parliamentary reserve'. This does not amount to a power of veto, and the extent to which governments in the past fully respected the right to consultation is open to question.

The current government is committed to effective scrutiny by Parliament of proposals emanating from each of the three pillars of the European Union.[27] It provides Parliament with copies of proposed European legislation and other proposals which may have important policy, legislative or financial implications. Each is accompanied by an explanatory memorandum explaining both the document and the government's views on it. The documents may then be considered both by the Commons European Legislative Committee and the Lords European Communities Committee, a sub-committee of which may carry out an inquiry on proposals which have particular importance. The Lords committee is particularly influential. The government responds in writing to its reports and, in the case of its sub-committee E on Law and Institutions, the letters are collected and published twice a year. Neither the Commons nor Lords committee has a mandate to consider the impact of the proposals on the UK's international human rights obligations.

No committee in either House has a remit to report on treaties negotiated outside of the framework of the European Union. The Lords Liaison Committee is currently considering a proposal from a number of peers including Lord Lester to establish a Treaties Committee (or sub-committee) to perform that function. Their memorandum, *Parliamentary scrutiny of non-EU treaties* (January 1999) argues that treaties no longer deal only with matters of foreign relations, defence and trade but with such aspects of modern life as transport, human rights, policing and social policy. In those circumstances it argues that it is necessary for Parliament to have a voice, as is the case in the majority of OECD countries in relation to at least some categories of treaty.

Conclusion

Scrutiny of legislative proposals within Whitehall has been developed around 'Strasbourg proofing', a modest, administrative procedure designed to reduce the risk of adverse findings under the ECHR. This process has never aimed to promote a higher profile for human rights throughout government nor to draw attention to all of the UK's international human rights obligations. A lack of transparency has enabled Ministers to ignore advice that legislation or policy breached the Convention. Innovations in policy appraisal in Northern Ireland illustrate how a more systematic and structured approach to scrutiny might be fashioned.

Although Parliament has developed effective scrutiny in other areas (such as in the work of the House of Lords European Communities Committee) assessment of primary or secondary legislation for its conformity with the UK's human rights obligations remains unsystematic and without any focus. Past practice offers important lessons to those now determining new procedures linked to the Human Rights Act: human rights have enjoyed a low priority within Parliament as a whole and both Houses have lacked the necessary expertise to probe and challenge Ministers. Future arrangements need to equip members with expert advice and assistance and ensure that informed opinions on compliance with international standards produced within Parliament carry greater authority.

Scrutiny arrangements can make an important contribution to better government. They can help to produce clearer law; save the time, expense and disruption resulting from successful court challenges to the validity of policy or legislation and can improve the accountability and openness of government and law-making processes.

Endnotes

1.   Klug F, Starmer K and Weir S (1996) *The Three Pillars of Liberty: Political Rights and Freedoms in the United Kingdom* Routledge.

2.   The first, 'Reducing the Risk of Legal Challenge' is dated March 1987, and the second, 'The Judge over your Shoulder – Judicial

Review of Administrative Decisions' is dated 6 July 1987. For a general commentary on these memoranda see Bradley A 'The Judge Over Your Shoulder' [1987] *Public Law* 485, and 'Protecting Government Decisions from Legal Challenge' [1988] *Public Law* 1.

3. Office of Public Service, Cabinet Office, November 1996, Appendix E. The Guide states that any request for advice should be copied to the Legal Secretariat of the Law Officers, the Lord Advocate's Department, the Home Office, the Scottish Office Home Department and the Northern Ireland Office.

4. Cabinet Office (1997) *Questions of Procedure for Ministers* Cabinet Office.

5. Kinley, D, 'Parliamentary Scrutiny for Human Rights Compliance: a duty neglected?' in Alston, P, *Promoting Human Rights through Bills of Rights* (forthcoming, 1999), Oxford University Press, p111.

6. See also consideration of impact of ECHR on proposals for new community treatment orders (DoH (1993) *Legal Powers on the Care of Mentally Ill People in the Community: Report of the Internal Review* DoH); or of ECHR on proposals for new laws on mental incapacity (LCD (1997) *Who Decides? Making decisions on behalf of mentally-incapacitated adults* TSO, paragraph 2.15.

7. 'Mainstreaming' is the term used mainly within EU institutions to refer to sex equality proofing in relation to policy-making and service delivery.

8. See annual reports obtainable from Central Community Relations Unit, Northern Ireland Office.

9. Committee on the Administration of Justice (1996) *Fair Employment for All* CAJ.

10. McCrudden C (1996) *Mainstreaming Fairness? A discussion paper on 'Policy Appraisal and Fair Treatment'* CAJ; Committee on the Administration of Justice (1996) *Fair Employment for All* CAJ.

11. The NIO has been criticised by the Equal Opportunities Commission for Northern Ireland for its promotion of privatisation policies seen to have a differential adverse impact on women public sector workers. Although the PAFT guidelines would appear to rule out economic and industrial policies having such an effect, the previous government persisted with them despite clear evidence of unfairness.

12. Standing Advisory Commission on Human Rights (1997) *Employment Equality: Building for the Future* Stationery Office.

13. Northern Ireland Office (1998) *Partnership for Equality: the government's proposals for future legislation and policies on Employment Equality in Northern Ireland* Cm 3890 TSO.

14. *Ibid* paragraph 4.7.

15. See s.68-78 and Schedules 7, 8 and 9, Northern Ireland Act 1998.

16. This term means any Public General Act; Local and Personal Act; Private Act; Church of England Measure; Order in Council made under the Northern Ireland Constitution Act 1973 or under the Royal Prerogative. We concentrate on Public General Acts.

17. For example, the Foreign Affairs Committee's inquiry into the introduction of the controversial 'primary purpose' rule affecting the grant of visas to married applicants or those intending marriage.

18. See for example debates on Drug Trafficking Offences Act 1986 and the case of Welch -v- United Kingdom (1995) Series A, no 307-A, where the European Court of Human Rights found the Act imposed a retrospective criminal penalty.

19. Such as the Counsel's opinion and briefing supplied by Liberty to peers involved in the debates on the Security Services Bill during 1996.

20. The Commonwealth Immigrants Act 1968 took less than a week to complete all its stages. The European Commission on Human Rights found it violated Articles 3, 8 and 14 of the ECHR and the government was forced to introduce amending legislation.

21. For illustrations of these points see debates on Contempt of Court Act 1981, Criminal Justice and Public Order Act 1994, Security Services Act 1996 and Asylum and Immigration Act 1996.

22. See debates on Commonwealth Immigrants Act 1968, Criminal Justice and Public Order Act 1994, Police Act 1997.

23. This definition includes any Order in Council not made in exercise of the Royal Prerogative or under the Northern Ireland Constitution Act 1973; any order, rules, regulations, scheme, warrant, bylaw or other instrument made under primary legislation.

24. House of Commons Select Committee on Procedure (1996) *Delegated Legislation Session 1995-96 Fourth Report* HMSO.

25. This figure excludes the *Soering* case (Series A, no 161, 7 July 1989) as the Court in that case found only a potential violation which did not actually occur.

26. HC Debs, vol 831, cols 274-5

27. See *The Scrutiny of European Union Business* Cm 4095 November
     1998.

4. An agenda for reform

The government recognises the need to strengthen Whitehall procedures to ensure thorough compliance with the Human Rights Act and is taking steps to do so.[1] MPs and peers are also expected to participate more directly in the process of scrutiny and in raising the profile of human rights in Parliament.

This chapter sets out the objectives for reform and how they might be accomplished. After outlining some principles to guide the necessary changes we describe a programme of possible options for the government. In Whitehall they are centred on a new procedure for assessing the impact of policy and legislation on human rights, and in Parliament on the role of a multi-functional Human Rights Committee. Although the focus is on Whitehall and Westminster, the approach advocated is equally applicable to the devolved executives and the Parliament and Assemblies in Scotland, Northern Ireland and Wales respectively.

Objectives

The new procedures in Whitehall and in Westminster should be designed to achieve three principal objectives:

- to ensure compliance of domestic law, policy and practice with the standards in the European Convention and compliance with wider international human rights conventions binding on the UK;

- to promote good practice throughout the public sector;

- to identify opportunities in policy and legislation to extend human rights protection and to promote greater respect for human rights and the responsibilities they entail.

The first objective represents the minimum response required in light of incorporation of the ECHR. The second and third objectives complement it, reflecting the spirit of the legislation and the government's intention that the Act should foster a culture of rights.

Compliance

Procedures in Whitehall and Parliament must at least be designed to limit the occasions when government is found by the UK courts, or the European Court of Human Rights, to have failed to uphold ECHR standards in its policies or proposals for legislation or in the exercise of its discretionary powers. For government is bound to find itself exposed to challenge with greater frequency, and in a wider range of situations, when the Human Rights Act is brought into force in the year 2000.

Public law proceedings and the scope of judicial review will be extended as the rights in the Convention become enforceable, and the principle of proportionality is introduced. Faced with this challenge, officials throughout Whitehall need to be freshly equipped to understand the implications of the ECHR for new policy and legislation so that they consistently meet its enforceable standards. Just as the existing guidance is designed to avoid the risk of challenge at the European Court of Human Rights, so the revised guidance must enable officials to minimise the risk of challenge in the UK's domestic courts and tribunals.

Good practice

One of the government's ambitions for the Human Rights Act is that it will foster a culture of rights and responsibilities.[2] By this it means greater awareness of, and respect for, fundamental human rights and the responsibilities they entail in all areas of our lives. Ensuring that legislation and policy comply with the minimum standards upheld by the courts will not, in itself, achieve that objective. Government must consider how policy could go beyond compliance to build human rights objectives into the policy making process, identifying its goal not as compliance but as good practice.

Opportunities to extend human rights protection

Procedures could be directed solely at existing policy and legislative proposals, in order to ensure compliance and good practice. However, government could go one step further and ask departments to identify new opportunities to further human rights protection or to raise awareness of human rights principles and the mutual responsibilities they entail. In this case, officials would not only draw up a human rights impact assessment for existing initiatives, but would be pro-active in suggesting positive new steps which the government could take. Such initiatives could be co-ordinated or monitored by a central unit. It is only if the government adopts this option that it could be said to be developing a strategy for extending human rights protection, rather than the more limited option of assessing the impact of existing proposals.

In order to achieve these three objectives, it is clear from our review of existing procedures in Whitehall and Parliament that:

- Scrutiny needs to become a more *proactive* process, and one that is capable of influencing the development of policy, procedures and law earlier in their design and drafting.

- The emphasis within the scrutiny process must change from prevention and the avoidance of risk to a *goal-oriented* process which reflects the government's positive responsibility to uphold its obligation, under international law, to guarantee the body of international human rights standards to all its citizens.

- The government should learn from parallel initiatives which have been established to achieve positive goals across government such as the use, and central monitoring, of impact assessments; the Policy Assessment and Fair Treatment procedures in Northern Ireland; and commitment to publishing departmental information on objectives, targets and performance.

- Scrutiny must involve a significant level of *expertise* – providing decision-makers with timely, accurate and relevant legal and other information on issues of compliance and good practice.

- The scrutiny process should be more *transparent*, reflecting Ministers' desire to promote a new culture of openness in government. Elected representatives and the public will then be able to assess the reasons for decisions and hold accountable those responsible for scrutiny on their behalf.

- The present approach lacks structure and consistency causing difficulties which we have highlighted. In future, procedures must be, and be seen to be, more rigorous and systematic with *clearer outcomes*, some of which can be *evaluated* – such as minimising the cost of successful challenges to government decisions, under the Human Rights Act.

- Procedures should not be restricted to assessing the impact of existing proposals but identify new opportunities to extend human rights protection or to raise awareness.

- Changes to policy and procedure must be *practical and viable*. New methods of scrutiny and accountability which are inordinately cumbersome and inflexible will discredit the new approach if they are seen to delay the government's legislative programme.[3]

In practical terms, there are three new kinds of procedures needed to which these objectives should be applied:

Impact assessments

- More effective scrutiny in Whitehall and Westminster of Bills and secondary legislation both for conformity to the ECHR (and wider international human rights standards binding on the United Kingdom) and to implement good practice.

- Effective scrutiny of *existing* legislation, policy and practice against the same standards.

Remedial order procedure

- A Parliamentary procedure to deal with government proposals to amend existing legislation following a court declaration under s.4 Human Rights Act that the legislation in question is incompatible with the ECHR.

Treaty making and monitoring

- Closer Parliamentary involvement in a decision that the UK should sign an international human rights treaty and any decision to derogate from, or enter reservations to, that treaty.

- Closer Parliamentary involvement in any subsequent process of reporting on the UK's compliance with such treaties to the international supervisory body which monitors compliance with the Convention's standards.

Reform in Whitehall

The government recognises that 'Strasbourg proofing' needs to be replaced with a more rigorous assessment of compliance with the ECHR and has instructed officials to report on that assessment when collective approval for a new policy is sought, not only when approval is subsequently sought for a Bill.[4] Under s.19 of the Human Rights Act, Ministers must publish a statement on the compatibility of each Bill with the ECHR before Second Reading and it has been agreed that the statement will be published on the face of the Bill. The government rejected a proposal made during the debates on the Human Rights Bill that the statement include the reasoning behind it. The intention is thus that the human rights impact assessment drawn up by officials, on the basis of legal advice, will remain confidential. The government also rejected the idea that there be a single Minister responsible for ensuring that departments carried out their impact assessments effectively, or that a central unit should be established for that purpose. As yet it is unclear whether the government intends to adopt a narrow compliance strategy or to take steps which will ensure the pursuit of good practice.

We propose that Whitehall adopts an approach to human rights impact assessments, and introduces procedures, designed to ensure consistency across government. The goal of the Cabinet Office guidance should, first, not simply be designed to guarantee compliance with the legally enforceable provisions of the Human Rights Act. It should also aim to encourage, in the planning and formulation of new policy, a closer attention to the opportunities to promote human rights protection and, in turn, to the contribution which human rights standards can make to good government and better administrative practice. Such assessments, when combined with clear leadership at a Ministerial and official level, and a new openness derived from annual reporting, could transform the dry task of testing for legal compliance into an influence more dynamic and innovative.

At present, the Foreign and Commonwealth Office is the only department to have built human rights objectives into policy formulation. Its *Guidelines to Posts and Departments* on Human Rights in Foreign Policy, under the heading *Mainstreaming*, state:

> Ministers are concerned that human rights should be integrated into policy-making at all levels.

The intention, in relation to the development of policy concerning individual countries, is that:

> human rights issues are looked at alongside other political, economic and security issues and not as a 'bolt-on'.[5]

Impact assessments

The idea of incorporating impact assessments into the policy making process is gaining wider recognition. As we noted in Chapter 2, the UN Committee which monitors the UK's compliance with the Convention on Economic, Social and Cultural Rights, recently recommended that:

> consideration be given to the requirement that a human rights assessment or impact statement be made an integral part of every proposed piece of legislation or policy initiative on a basis analogous to environmental impact assessments or statements.[6]

To improve the responsiveness of policy making to important principles or interests 'impact assessments' are indeed often now required. They have become an accepted way of ensuring that policy is better able to meet the full range of government objectives, with substantial guidance given to officials on how to carry it out, including general guidance from the Treasury,[7] from the Cabinet Office on regulatory appraisal,[8] the Department of Health on health appraisal[9] and the Cabinet Office, Home Office and DfEE on policy appraisal for equal treatment.[10]

Equal treatment

Impact assessments have been required for some years in Britain in relation to equal treatment on grounds of race, gender, disability and age, but have not been widely carried out in practice in most departments, perhaps due to a lack of priority accorded to them at ministerial level, to date, and hence the lack of any central enforcement mechanism. In an attempt to breath fresh life into the approach, fresh guidance was issued in November 1998. *Policy Appraisal for Equal Treatment*, which requires impact assessments to be made on grounds of race, gender, disability and age, states:

> Government departments must take full account of the needs and experiences of all those affected by their policies. We must understand how policy can have a different impact on different groups in society. We have to bring this understanding to policy developments and work to ensure that the results are fair, lawful and practical, and promote equal opportunities in the widest sense...

> Policy appraisal is both common sense and good practice. You and your Ministers need to know how your policies and programmes will affect the public and you need to make sure that they comply with the law. But policy appraisal is not just about the law; it is about good government... Unless you find out about the impact on different groups, you cannot be sure whether policies are having the effect government intends. Once you have analysed the impact of your policies then you need to decide what to do about any adverse differential impacts.

The guidance draws officials' attention to the relevant domestic anti-discrimination law and notes:

> The UK is also a signatory to a large number of international conventions which have anti-discrimination provisions; although these do not currently provide a right of individual complaint against the UK, policy should be informed by an awareness of the UK's international obligations.

Finally, the guidance requires that the results of impact assessments should always be brought to the attention of Ministers but there is no requirement to identify the results of the assessments when proposals are put up for Cabinet approval, nor to refer to them in the department's annual report.

Policy appraisal for fair treatment

As discussed in Chapter 3, a not-dissimilar process was introduced in Northern Ireland in 1994 to assess policy proposals against a set of 'fair treatment' guidelines. The results were collated and published annually in a report by the Secretary of State. Now a new statutory duty is to be imposed on public authorities to promote equality of opportunity and to set out how they will do so in a published statutory scheme, monitored by the new Equality Commission. Public authorities, including government departments, will be obliged to consult affected groups – which include the elderly, homosexuals and adults with dependants as well as, for instance, minority communities – and be expected to make clear what impact fair treatment considerations had on the refinement of policy options.

Environmental impact assessments

A further example is environmental impact assessments, introduced by the last government in 1991[11] and reinforced in 1998 with new guidance after a review carried out by KPMG found that departments needed to take a more systematic approach to assessing the environmental impact of policy initiatives. The guidance, *Policy appraisal and the Environment*, describes environmental appraisal as 'part of the overall policy appraisal process that is being developed across government' and as one means to achieve the government's manifesto commitment to 'put the environment at the heart of decision making'.[12] The guidance states that assessing the effect of a policy or programme on the environment means considering the *outcome* of that policy, not only the immediate *output*. The aim should be to maximise benefits to the environment and to minimise costs. The appraisal should be part of the policy development process from the beginning, built into the assessment of alternative options, not an after-thought once the preferred options have been identified and the policy is well developed. Departments are encouraged to consult on the potential impact of policies and to publish their appraisals. Where 'costs' are unavoidable, mitigation measures may need to be considered to offset the impact of the policy. Finally, the department must put in place arrangements for monitoring and evaluating the policy once implemented.

In order to ensure that this approach receives the priority it needs, each department has a 'Green' Minister responsible for ensuring that the necessary systems are in place. He or she is a member of a Cabinet Committee on the Environment, chaired by the Deputy Prime Minister. Those Ministers also report to the Interdepartmental Environmental Audit Select Committee established in the House of Commons to monitor Whitehall's compliance with these procedures.

Freedom of information

Following the 1998 White Paper,[13] Ministers will introduce draft legislation to establish new enforceable duties on government and other public authorities to disclose information to the public. This opens up the business of government in a fundamental way, rendering Ministers and officials more accountable for decisions, policies and proposals and the reasons for them. Prior to any legislation requiring this, Departments are already using annual reports, websites and other means to convey to the public more information on their key objectives, targets, activity and performance.

Whitehall strategy

Drawing on these approaches, we suggest that the government needs to introduce procedures within departments, and a Ministerial network between departments, to put human rights at the heart of government decision-making.

The key components of the new approach would be as follows:

- Cabinet Office Guidance on *Human Rights Impact Assessments*.

- Leadership and co-ordination in implementing the new policy and procedures established across government at Ministerial level.

- A central unit to advise departments and co-ordinate the human rights strategy and impact assessments.

- An annual human rights report, matching that already produced on human rights in foreign policy.

- The production and regular updating of a human rights manual for common use throughout Whitehall.

Cabinet Office guidance

Appraisals of new policy or proposals for legislation will be carried out in future in accordance with guidance issued by the Cabinet Office. The first objective of that guidance will be to ensure that proposed policy and legislation complies with the standards in the ECHR so that it is not open to challenge under the Human Rights Act.

It is our view that the guidance should not only address the pressing needs created by the Human Rights Act, however, but take account of the full scope and range of the UK's international obligations. 'Strasbourg proofing' will thus cease to be a suitable term to describe the scrutiny process and we propose that the term Human Rights Impact Assessment (HRIA) be used instead.

The HRIA Guidance would summarise the aims of scrutiny, to secure compliance and good practice, and methods to be used to achieve it. The task would be assisted by the production and regular updating of a human rights manual, along the lines described below.

We described in Chapter 3 the process of scrutiny for compliance with the ECHR: the questions which need to be asked, and the tests applied, when considering the effect of policy or legislation on *absolute rights, rights with defined exemptions* and *qualified rights*. The guidance would explain this process and should summarise the broad principles drawn from relevant international caselaw and jurisprudence to assist in interpreting what is permitted. Where it is necessary to determine whether a proposed restriction on a right is proportionate and necessary, the Guidance should advise officials to consider consulting outside expertise and representatives of those working in the relevant field.

Most proposals for policy or law will not involve any restriction of any right protected under the ECHR. Here, scrutiny would have two additional purposes. Occasionally, what is suggested will fail to meet a standard required under another binding Convention, such as the ICCPR or CRC, which are not enforceable in the UK. The non-discrimination provisions of the former, for example, are wider than the very limited protection from non-discrimination found in the European Convention and the ECHR contains little of specific relevance to the situation of children. Here, the aim of the impact assessment would be to identify where government policy might fall short of the standard required. Such a step has particular importance for the regular monitoring of the UN Conventions undertaken by the UN Committees set up for that purpose.

Secondly, where there was no possibility of a breach of any Convention, the assessment would offer the opportunity for the promotion and development of better practice and a more explicit culture of rights and responsibilities. This would prepare government and public authorities for the possibility of higher enforceable standards in the future as ECHR jurisprudence evolves.

Taking this broader view, for example:

- The Department for Education and Employment could, when considering reform of the curriculum to incorporate education for citizenship, consider the relevance and importance of a human rights component and the opportunity provided by the change to promote the teaching of human rights principles in schools.[14]

- Department of Health policy on the use of the Mental Health Act and its Code of Practice could explicitly raise the importance of human rights issues in the treatment of detained psychiatric patients – not explicitly required under current ECHR jurisprudence but in line with evolving principles. Policy in the field of genetic testing and concerning the control of personal health information could also be informed by human rights principles setting standards above and beyond the strict requirements of the ECHR.

- In guidance to improve the treatment of vulnerable witnesses or parties, the Lord Chancellor's Department could promote the relevance of human rights to a fair hearing.

- Efforts by the Department for Culture, Media and Sport in co-operation with the Press Complaints Commission to reduce the portrayal of derogatory racial stereotypes in the national print media could be explicitly reinforced by reference to CERD.

Even if the European Convention were to be the yardstick rather than wider international standards, it is clear that the discriminatory impact of any proposals would have to be considered and the potential for promoting equality. This suggests that human rights impact assessments should not be separate from policy assessment for fair treatment but that the two procedures should be developed together.

Existing legislation

When the New Zealand government introduced its Human Rights Act in 1993, a statutory duty was placed on the Human Rights Commission to scrutinise all existing legislation within New Zealand to ensure that it complied with the Act.[15] Known as *Consistency 2000*, the exercise was required to be completed by the end of December 1998 so that any legislative reform required to comply with the Act could be completed by the beginning of the year 2000. From that date, all past as well as future legislation would be required to comply with the Human Rights Act. The Human Rights Commission co-ordinated a scrutiny exercise, in which the ground-work was largely carried out by officials within government departments, and duly reported its findings to the government at the end of last year.

The UK government has decided not to carry out an exercise on this scale but has, through a letter in November 1998 from the Home Office Permanent Secretary to the heads of all other government departments, asked officials to draw to the government's attention any provisions in existing legislation which could breach the Human Rights Act. If this exercise is to be effective, the guidance should advise departments to focus on those Acts and secondary legislation most likely to lead to a breach; that is, a strategic rather than a comprehensive approach, given that no additional resources have been allocated to this task. To the extent that potential breaches can be identified and remedied at this stage, the government will avoid subsequent challenge in the courts. It is a necessary prevention strategy which should be accorded some priority.

Leadership at a Ministerial level

In order to ensure that the changes proposed are given priority and that implementation is championed within government as a whole, we propose that a named Minister be given responsibility for ensuring that the Act is implemented successfully across government. This suggestion was considered by Ministers at the time of publication of *Rights Brought Home* but was rejected.[16] The importance of the new policy and its consequences for Whitehall should cause the government to reconsider its position.

The Home Office might seem the obvious location, given its role in guiding the Human Rights Act through Parliament and the fact that the Home Office is responsible for some of the most problematic areas of policy such as immigration and criminal justice. For the latter reason, its Ministers may have a particular concern to ensure that the new Guidance is fully implemented. There is a Human Rights Unit established within the department, currently responsible for managing implementation of the Act, with appropriate expertise. Against this option, it could be argued that the lead Minister should be independent of the government department the activities or policies of which may be most likely to attract challenges under the Human Rights Act.

The alternative option would be a Cabinet Office Minister. There may be some merit in considering this alternative given the involvement of the Cabinet Office in drawing up the necessary guidance, its general responsibility for the Civil Service and the way in which the department works to co-ordinate initiatives across Whitehall, for example, on social exclusion, better regulation and better government initiatives such as Service First. It is a Cabinet Ministerial sub-committee (of the Constitution Reform Policy Committee) which has overseen introduction of the Human Rights Act (CRP(EC)). An inter-departmental committee of officials, CRP(EC)O, works to that sub-committee.

Regardless of the department in which the Minister is based, he or she should be supported by a unit tasked, first, with ensuring that HRIAs are carried out effectively across government. As in the Better Regulation Unit (now Regulatory Impact Unit), the impact assessments attached to all policy proposals submitted for collective agreement should be seen by the unit and signed off by the responsible Minister. Secondly, the unit should be responsible for developing proposals for a cross-government strategy on human rights, drawing on and responding to proposals coming forward from departments. Finally, it should have responsibility for compiling an annual *Human Rights Report* (see below).

Ministerial sponsors

The changes which were introduced in the Cabinet Office in 1998, including the formation of the Performance Innovation Unit to improve co-ordination across government, reflected recognition that new mechanisms are needed to deliver reforms which cut across more than one government department. Experience suggests that simply having a strong Ministerial lead from one department, even if it is the Cabinet Office, may not be sufficient to ensure that the issue is given priority within each department.

One way of overcoming this difficulty is for a Minister within each department to be given responsibility for ensuring that his or her department does implement the policy, or reforms, effectively. The 'Greening Government' initiative, as we have suggested, is an example of that approach, each departmental Minister reporting to a Cabinet sub-committee on the steps which have been taken to 'green' that department. Given the importance to the government of ensuring that each department does introduce effective scrutiny procedures and, we suggest, measures to promote a culture of rights, appointing Ministerial sponsors within each department would appear to be a necessary minimum step to achieve that objective. Each Minister should then ensure that there is a structure in place at official level within the department to deliver the dual objectives of scrutiny for compliance and, where appropriate, the achievement of positive human rights objectives.

Overseas experience

In devising such a structure it may be instructive to examine the approach taken in countries in which pre-legislative scrutiny procedures are already in place, albeit that, at this stage, those systems appear designed to ensure compliance rather than good practice. In Canada, for instance, the Minister of Justice is required to 'examine every Bill...to determine whether any of the provision thereof are inconsistent with the purposes and provisions of [the 1982 Charter of Rights and the 1960 Bill of Rights]. Regulations are similarly scrutinised and, where any inconsistency is found, the Minister must report to Parliament at the earliest opportunity'.[17]

In New Zealand, a pre-legislative scrutiny system for compliance with the Bill of Rights Act 1990 was established in 1991. S.7 of the Act requires the Attorney General to report to Parliament on any provision within a government Bill 'that appears to be inconsistent with any of the rights and freedoms contained in the Bill of Rights'. Guidance has been issued to all departments on assessing the implications of the Bill of Rights for their work. Only three Bills have yet been referred by the Attorney General to Parliament under these provisions. On two occasions, Parliament considered the limitations on rights to be acceptable; on the third occasion it did not proceed with the legislation. While both the Canadian and New Zealand systems are considered to have value, the fact that Ministers are unlikely ever to advise Parliament that a government Bill restricting rights is not justified, reinforces the need for the executive's scrutiny process to be mirrored, and its conclusions challenged, by Parliament.[18]

Annual Report

Parliament, the public and interested organisations should be regularly informed of the results of the assessments which are undertaken by each department, including the reasoning behind any s.19 statements (subject to the confidentiality of legal advice). To that end, each department should report annually to the central unit on the human rights impact of the department's initiatives during the year, and the steps taken by the department to promote human rights and equality. A summary of that information should also be included in each department's annual report.

An annual Human Rights Report should then be collated and published, setting out the impact of government initiatives throughout the year on human rights in the United Kingdom,[19] complementing the annual report already produced on human rights in foreign policy. By agreement with the newly devolved executives, it could potentially include chapters reporting on HRI assessments and initiatives in Scotland, Northern Ireland and Wales. This would enable the reader to grasp the impact of practice across departmental boundaries and enable good practice to be readily appreciated and shared.

The annual report would be presented to Parliament and examined by the Human Rights Committee. The committee might be expected to question Ministers on the contribution of their department.

A new Human Rights Manual

The proposed Cabinet Office guidance will necessarily focus primarily on the standards in the European Convention. Wider guidance is necessary on the full range of the UK's obligations under international human rights law, if officials are to be expected to show an appropriate awareness of those standards. We propose that a comprehensive human rights manual should be produced and distributed to all government departments and agencies to explain what the international human rights standards are, how they are enforced at national and international level and how they can help to develop better practice and policy in government. A manual of this kind is already produced for Foreign Office officials and diplomats. The manual could be a loose-leaf production so that it could be revised regularly as new agreements are ratified or reports on UK practice issued by the UN supervisory bodies.

Over time, once the Parliamentary Human Rights Committee is well established, the manual could incorporate the practice in Australia where, since 1989, a *Legislative Scrutiny Manual* has provided guidance to officials on the responsibilities and expectations of the Parliamentary committees responsible for scrutinising primary and secondary legislation (see below). The manual indicates how the committee applies the principles in its terms of reference and the approach it has taken in relation to specific issues.[20]

Reform in Westminster

In Chapter 3 we showed that Parliament currently lacks any systematic approach to monitoring legislation for conformity to human rights standards. This has led in the past to it remaining ignorant of some of the human rights implications of proposed legislation or unable to develop its concerns so as to challenge proposals successfully before they are approved. One reason for this has been an acknowledged lack of expertise which has inhibited MPs from speaking with authority on matters of legislative compliance with international human rights law.

Reforming Parliament's role in promoting human rights scrutiny and accountability will fall into five principal areas of responsibility. These are the following:

● Scrutiny of primary legislation

● Consideration of government proposals for Remedial Orders following a Declaration of Incompatibility or an adverse ruling from the European Court of Human Rights

● Scrutiny of delegated legislation

● Monitoring existing policy and practice for compliance with the ECHR and wider international standards

● Involvement in treaty ratification and reports to UN supervisory bodies.

In the context of the Human Rights Act, the government itself proposed that Parliament should establish a new committee. The Lord Chancellor, Lord Irvine:

> We are attracted to the idea of a parliamentary committee on human rights... It would be a natural focus for the increased interest in human rights issues which Parliament will inevitably take when we have brought rights home. It could, for example, not only keep the protection of human rights under review, but could also be in the forefront of public education and consultation on human rights. It could receive written submissions and hold public hearings at a number of locations across the country. It could be in the van [sic] of the promotion of a human rights culture across the country.[21]

The Home Secretary developed the point at a later stage in the Bill's passage through the House, arguing that the role of a Human Rights Committee could be to:

monitor progress in implementing the Act and the way in which
it develops and, where appropriate, to make recommendations
to Parliament for changes that may be needed.[22]

Fiona Mactaggart MP added her own suggestions on the
committee's potential role. In addition to assessing the impact of Bills
on human rights and agreeing that it should contribute to public
education, she argued that the committee should oversee public access
to legal representation in taking cases under the Act and should consider
whether the UK should sign up to international human rights standards
which it has not yet ratified.[23]

It was announced on 14 December 1998 that Parliament will
establish a Joint Human Rights Committee (of both Houses of
Parliament) during 1999, the functions of which, in general terms, will
be to conduct inquiries into human rights issues, scrutinise Remedial
Orders, examine draft legislation and consider whether the UK needs a
Human Rights Commission.[24] The Committee's precise terms of
reference have not yet been decided, including, for instance, whether it
will be responsible for scrutinising secondary legislation such as
statutory instruments and whether it will have any role in relation to the
ratification and monitoring of international treaties. In the following
analysis of the roles Parliament now needs to play, we shall indicate the
unique contribution which we consider the Committee should make.

Scrutiny of primary legislation

How should primary legislation be scrutinised in Parliament for its
conformity to the ECHR and wider international human rights
standards? Can this be achieved by building on current procedures and
practices and without causing unnecessary delays and complications?
These questions raise two quite separate practical questions:

- by what means, and at what stage, should MPs and peers be
  notified that legislation which is to be introduced in Parliament
  raises human rights issues?

- by what means should Parliament itself scrutinise such legislation
  in order to express a view on the question of its conformity to the
  ECHR and/or other relevant standards?

Identification of human rights issues

S.19 of the Human Rights Act requires any Bill, before its Second Reading, to be accompanied by a Ministerial statement containing the government's view on its compatibility with the provisions of the ECHR. The government has said that its practice will be for the statement to be printed on the face of the Bill and reproduced in the explanatory notes which accompanying it.

This is a significant step forward and provides the *opportunity* to enhance Parliament's consideration of the meaning and effect of legislative proposals. Where Whitehall's human rights impact assessment has uncovered the likelihood of an infringement, then this should be highlighted in the s.19 statement. There will thus be formal opportunities for members of both Houses to question Ministers as to the basis for their statement either that the Bill is compatible or, despite the fact that it may not be, that the government nevertheless wants Parliament to proceed.

For all that this procedure offers a great improvement on past practice, it has some limitations. The Act does not *require* the Ministerial statement to be incorporated as a memorandum into the Bill and it must only be made *before* the Second Reading of the Bill – no minimum period of time is specified. Secondly, the government is not required to give reasons. Under s.19(2):

> The statement must be in writing and be published in such manner as the Minister making it considers appropriate.

Finally, no provision is made for reassessing the s.19 statement if the Bill is substantially amended during its passage through the House.

Since the statement only concerns compatibility with the ECHR, Parliament will not discover if any of the proposed legislation is incompatible with other Convention standards, such as those in the ICCPR. Moreover, we fear that the statutory procedure – although it imposes a significant discipline upon Ministers and their officials – may provide Parliament with little more actual information than it currently learns when a Minister in charge of a Bill states his or her view, during debate, that legislation complies with the ECHR.

Explanatory memorandum

We propose that the Bill should be accompanied by a summary of the results of its Human Rights Impact Assessment (HRIA), much in the same way as it currently has to be accompanied by details of the financial implications of the Bill, its effects on public service manpower and the costs for business associated with compliance.

The summary could be in two parts: the first would relate to the ECHR and would constitute the s.19 statement. The second would refer to any other relevant international human rights standards and state how these relate to the provisions of the Bill.

The explanatory memorandum would not reveal the contents of confidential legal advice given to Ministers but would do more than simply state the Minister's opinion on the whole Bill. It would pinpoint those areas of the Bill which were thought to raise the possibility of a breach, the relevant provisions of the ECHR or other Convention and the position adopted by the government in relation to these: that is, either that no breach would follow from the provisions of the Bill or why the government intended to proceed with the legislation nevertheless.

A 'nevertheless' statement: additional measures

On the rare occasions that a Bill includes such a 'nevertheless' statement, we propose that additional procedural rules should apply. First, there should be a minimum period of delay between publication of the Bill and its Second Reading to permit members of the House in which it is introduced to register the impact of the government's statement, research the effects of the proposed legislation and prepare for the debate. A period of one month would be sufficient and Parliament's standing orders should be altered to provide for this.

Secondly, where a Bill is accompanied by such a statement then, by the government's own admission, the proposed legislation may be in breach of the UK's international legal obligations. Given the gravity of such a situation, we propose that the Bill should be time-tabled to ensure a full debate at each stage. Standing Orders should be amended to exclude that possibility of debates being inappropriately curtailed in the circumstances.

It may be argued that emergency circumstances sometimes require the abridgement of the time normally provided for the consideration of controversial legislation. If such an exception is to be permitted, then we propose that the law which results should only be in force for six months at most to allow for proper scrutiny to take place in the interim.

Private Members' Bills

Private Members' Bills are not subject to the s.19 procedure. No HRIA need therefore be carried out prior to their introduction in the House. We therefore suggest that, after Second Reading, the question of the Bill's compliance with the ECHR should be considered, as a matter of standing orders, before the Bill is allowed to proceed for consideration by the Standing Committee.

Options for scrutiny

The process of legislative scrutiny for human rights would involve some additional procedures being added to the current system. It would not replace that system but complement it, giving extra focus and attention to the wording and effect of a proposed measure which could restrict human rights.

As in Whitehall, the scrutiny of legislative proposals would begin by identifying those parts of a Bill which could restrict rights and which would require further consideration. The second step would consist of the technical, expert consideration of the wording of the proposed legislation and its probable effect. It would demand the application of recognised human rights legal principles and caselaw. The outcome of the process would be an opinion on the likelihood of breach not, at this stage, a substantive weighing up of the social or political justification for restricting the rights in question in order to secure the policy aims behind the legislation.

In relation to qualified rights, this stage might uncover the possibility of breach which could nevertheless be justified. In order to examine the grounds for this, a third – 'merits' – stage would be needed: a more in-depth examination of the political merits of the measure, its impact on those affected and its social context to arrive at a decision on its overall acceptability. It would be at this stage that the Parliamentarians would consider whether the measure was necessary for the 'prevention of crime' or 'national security', for instance, as required by the Convention, and proportional to that objective.

It will be especially important for Parliament to devote the time and resources to such additional scrutiny where the Ministerial statement discloses that the proposals may be incompatible with the Human Rights Act but that the government nevertheless wants Parliament to enact them.

In practice, as with the other scrutiny committees in Parliament such as the Delegated Powers and Deregulation Committee, each Bill would be scrutinised first not by the committee but by its clerks who must have the expertise to identify whether there are any issues of compliance which merit further consideration by the committee and a possible report to the House. The committee would thus focus its attention only on those sections of Bills which cause concern.

Once the potential for detailed scrutiny is established as part of the passage of legislation through Parliament, it is likely to have some restraining effect on a government's approach when introducing Bills. This has been the experience in the Australian National Parliament where the influential work of the Senate Committees responsible for scrutiny has discouraged the government from introducing legislation which is likely to be censored by either Senate Committee.

The Australian Parliament has pioneered scrutiny procedures through the work of two Senate committees: the Standing Committee for the Scrutiny of Bills (dealing with primary legislation) and the Standing Committee on Regulation and Ordinances (covering secondary legislation). The terms of reference of the committees require them to report on any provision in a Bill which, inter alia, 'trespass unduly on personal rights and liberties' and the impressive record of the former was influential in the decision in the UK in 1992 to set up the Select Committee on the Scrutiny of Delegated Powers, albeit not with the same terms of reference. A third body, the Sub-Committee on Human Rights of the Joint Standing Committee on Foreign Affairs, Defence and Trade reviews Australia's human rights record in both foreign and domestic policy and has produced a number of influential reports. It is expected to become a free-standing joint committee of Parliament.[25] The scrutiny committees are said to enjoy bi-partisan relations among their membership and to have a good working relationship with government under which Ministers respond to requests by the committee for comment on aspects of legislation which cause it concern.

It is noteworthy that the terms of reference of the scrutiny committees do not require them to use international human rights standards binding on Australia, such as the ICCPR, as their yardstick. Moreover, the requirement that the provisions trespass *unduly* on liberties has freed the committee to concur with infringements which might not be acceptable under that treaty. It is suggested that, for the committee to conduct a more effective scrutiny for compliance with international human rights standards, it would need to be supported by staff with appropriate human rights expertise or seek expert advice externally.[26] The Human Rights and Equal Opportunity Commission, established in 1986, can on occasion provide an expert opinion on draft legislation and policy and has done so to good effect on a number of occasions. However, its limited resources prevent it from scrutinising all federal legislative proposals which could give rise to breaches of Australia's international human right obligations.

Parliamentary Human Rights Committee

When the Human Rights Committee is given the task of scrutinising Bills for compliance with human rights standards, its work will not replace the existing Standing Committee system of deliberation on Bills, but complement it. The key question for the committee will be one of timing: how soon will it be notified of the intended content of a Bill so that it can consider it prior to debate in either house? Will it receive the Bill in time to comment before Second Reading, or prior to the detailed consideration of the Bill, clause by clause, by a committee of the House? If the Bill is subsequently amended, will the Committee be given a further opportunity to consider the compatibility with the ECHR of the clause in question?

Where the government's s.19 statement indicates that the Bill may not comply with the Convention, it will be particularly important that the Committee consider the relevant provisions of the Bill in detail, inviting submissions and drawing on outside evidence if necessary. We suggest that the Human Rights Committee be given the power to embark on such an inquiry. If established as a Joint Committee of both

Houses then it will still be practicable for members to investigate issues fully and report, albeit that the legislation may have passed from one House to be considered by the other. In that event, it should report before the Bill proceeds to Second Reading in the second House.

To ensure that scrutiny is conducted adequately without being squeezed out by ongoing inquiries, we suggest that the terms of reference for the Committee make clear that scrutiny of Bills should be a mandatory function, albeit that the Committee could determine to which Bills it should give its detailed attention. This role should be compatible with the other functions of the Committee, which we outline below, particularly if responsibility for scrutiny was to be delegated to a sub-committee established for this sole purpose. Preliminary scrutiny would, as we have suggested, be conducted by the Committee's expert staff who would draw to members' attention those Bills or parts of Bills that merit further consideration. This function would also complement the Committee's wider scrutiny and monitoring role, in relation to existing legislation and policy, and provide opportunities for members to increase their competence in and understanding of human rights law and practice.

Special Standing Committee

Where a Ministerial statement warns Parliament that the Bill could restrict human rights, the Human Rights Committee could recommend that the Bill be considered by a Special Standing Committee prior to its line by line examination. Such committees take written and oral evidence and provide opportunities for a detailed and open examination of the policy arguments for and against the legislation being passed in the form proposed.

To date the procedure has been little used but it would be appropriate. In 1982, a Special Standing Committee was used for the government's Mental Health (Amendment) Bill, enabling the civil liberties, social and ethical issues surrounding the proposed reforms to be fully canvassed, together with the professional, patient and public interest perspectives relevant to the changes proposed. This procedure is being used for the Immigration and Asylum Bill published in February 1999.

The reason that the procedure is little used results, in part, from the government's fear that it would unduly delay the legislative programme.

The government's ability to determine whether Special Standing Committees are established weighs the argument in favour of the Human Rights Committee having the principal responsibility for scrutiny as it will be able to decide when detailed consideration is necessary. Where a Special Standing Committee is established, there will be nothing to prevent it considering the human rights implications of the Bill within its inquiry.

Remedial Orders

Under the Human Rights Act, the UK's higher courts may declare legislation to be incompatible with the ECHR or, as has happened on a number of occasions in the past, the European Court of Human Rights may judge it to be in breach of the Convention. When this happens, the government can use the power in s.10 of the Act to make an Order to effect the necessary amendment. Compared with the time that primary legislation would usually take, this offers a fast-track procedure. In our view, the Committee should consider *any* legislation which the courts have declared incompatible, regardless of how the government decided to respond.

When the government chooses to use the fast-track procedure, Parliament will have 60 days in which to consider the wording of the proposed Remedial Order which will be subject to the affirmative resolution procedure. Except in urgent cases, the Order must be approved in draft by a resolution of each House of Parliament. Where not approved in draft, it will cease to have effect if not approved by both Houses of Parliament within 60 sitting days of it having been introduced.

Remedial orders will need to be carefully scrutinised by Parliament, prior to receiving an affirmative resolution. Of necessity, they will concern a fundamental human rights issue and could amend or repeal an existing Act of Parliament. Schedule 2 to the Human Rights Act was amended during the passage of the Bill to require that similar procedures be adopted by the Minister, when introducing a Remedial Order, to those followed by Ministers in relation to statutory instruments which amend or repeal legislation deemed to impose an unnecessary regulatory burden. Such instruments are considered by the Delegated Powers Scrutiny Committee (DPSC). The key elements of that procedure are that the Minister should demonstrate to the committee that he or she has consulted interested parties; that he provide an explanatory memoranda setting out the reasons for the instrument; that there be 60 days in which Parliament can consider the proposal and finally that the Minister shall have regard to any representations made by the committee.

Robert Blackburn argued recently that the Standing Orders of the Human Rights Committee must, like those for the DPSC, ensure that the committee has had an opportunity to consider the Order, and to report to Parliament, before any motion to affirm the order is considered by either House. Standing Orders should, for instance, require the Committee to report on a draft Order within a specified time after the Order is laid before the House; state that, where the committee recommends that the Order not be approved, no motion to approve the draft Order shall be made unless the House has previously resolved to disagree with the committee's report; and that a resolution to affirm an order shall be made before the committee has laid its report before the House, any motion relating to a report from the committee being given precedence in the day's order paper over a motion to approve the draft Order.[27]

The Committee should be notified by government in advance of any intention to make a Remedial Order under the Act and should have a duty to examine a draft of the instrument. It could recommend to both Houses that the proper course should be the conventional route for amending primary legislation, rather than by Remedial Order. Its recommendation might influence the outcome of a resolution to approve the Order. To reflect the way in which draft Statutory Instruments are currently considered within Parliament, and amendments sought from Ministers, the Human Rights Committee could be given the power to require the Minister to reconsider the wording of the draft instrument.

Scrutiny of delegated legislation

In view of the expected workload of the Human Rights Committee and the great quantity of statutory instruments now requiring scrutiny, some 1500 per annum, it is necessary to consider whether responsibility for examining them for human rights implications should fall to the Human

Rights Committee or whether the Joint Statutory Instruments Committee (JSIC) should have its standing orders extended to include scrutiny for compatibility with the Human Rights Act. This latter approach is recommended by Blackburn who suggests that the committee could appoint a sub-committee, taking on additional MPs and peers, for that purpose.[28]

The argument for using the JSIC is clearly that, where an instrument is already being scrutinised according to a specific set of criteria, it would take less time for that committee to add an additional set of criteria than for the Human Rights Committee to look at the instrument afresh. On the other hand, as the human rights implications of the instrument fall outside the current terms of reference of the committee, the staff assisting the committee would need to acquire expertise in the ECHR and human rights law. This would seem to be an unnecessary duplication of expertise. Moreover, if the Human Rights Committee is considering, or has considered, the parent Act – for instance the Immigration legislation under which Immigration Rules are made – their knowledge of the former is likely to assist their task in assessing the implications of the latter. In Australia, both the Queensland and Victoria scrutiny committees review both primary and secondary legislation.

On balance, we therefore suggest that the Human Rights Committee be given responsibility for scrutinising secondary legislation for compliance with the Human Rights Act, although there should be no objection to the terms of reference of the Statutory Instruments Committee also being amended to include that function, should that be proposed.

Monitoring government policy and practice

Scrutiny of legislation comprises only one part of the role of Parliament in upholding the rights of UK citizens. It must also monitor government policy and practice and hold Ministers to account for the exercise of their discretion. The UK's obligations under the ECHR and wider international standards needs to be part of that general oversight. Such scrutiny is the role pre-eminently of Parliament's Select Committee system, including the proposed Human Rights Committee.

Select Committees

Select Committees provide MPs and peers with an opportunity to examine the impact of government policy and practice in depth. One commentator has indicated their value in the following way:

> I would emphasise first, here speaking as one who has in the past given evidence on behalf of the government, that the value of the scrutiny process is in part that it forces those with more direct power to consider their positions and their arguments carefully and to defend them in the face of public questioning by a committee whose members may have long experience of the subject-matter involved.[29]

The existing Select Committee system has only been in place since 1979. In the House of Commons, Standing Orders have established that the remit of most Select Committees mirrors that of a government department or one part of it: the Select Committee on Health, Select Committee on Education and Employment, and so forth. The committees, responsible for examining the 'expenditure, administration and policy' of their respective department, are appointed for the life of a Parliament. They are made up only of back-bench MPs, and, like Standing Committees, they reflect the political complexion of the House (although the chairs of some Select Committees do come from the Opposition benches). Each committee is serviced by House of Commons clerks, and they also may appoint specialist advisers. Under similar arrangements, Select Committees also operate in the House of Lords.

Select Committees play a critical role in calling the Executive to account. They may examine any subject of their own choosing within their broad remit, which includes the power to consider the work of relevant public bodies or quangos. The regular appearance of Ministers for questioning before Committees has become an invaluable contribution to open government and to Parliamentary scrutiny of executive action.

Human Rights Committee

To date, no Select Committee has had terms of reference which make any reference to human rights or the UK's international human rights obligations. The Human Rights Committee will therefore be an entirely new departure. Parliament's capacity to monitor policy and practice in the field of domestic human rights will be vastly enhanced. As a Select Committee not linked to any departmental policy agenda, the Human Rights Committee would nevertheless operate along similar lines, deciding at the start of the session on a range of subjects to inquire into and report on. It should nevertheless have the flexibility to conduct an urgent investigation should this prove necessary.

The Committee should monitor how the Human Rights Act is working, including citizens' access to justice, and the extent to which existing policy and practice complies with the ECHR. It could consider the annual Human Rights Report from the government and ask Ministers to answer questions on their departmental record. Blackburn suggests that the committee would do well to scrutinise some existing statutes for compliance with the ECHR, or seek reports from departments on the results of their own compliance exercise, in order to avoid complaints of non compliance being resolved by litigation.[30] The Committee would have the powers needed to investigate a serious or systemic abuse of human rights, and from time to time, could undertake such an inquiry.

The Committee should also consider implementation of the other principal international standards binding on the UK. It might, for instance, take evidence on the extent to which the UK complies with the standards in the UN Convention on the Rights of the Child. Alternatively, if it were inquiring into the abuse of children's rights in a particular setting, it should take that Convention as a yardstick against which to measure the degree of protection afforded to children. Finally, in line with Labour's view in 1993 that incorporation of the ECHR should only be the first step towards the eventual adoption of a UK Bill of Rights,[31] the Committee could conduct an inquiry into the potential scope of that document.

To assist the Committee in these roles, and to link it with the public bodies already having some responsibility for human rights, the Data Protection Registrar, the EOC, the CRE and the new Disability Rights Commission could have a formal relationship with Committee. The Committee could receive regular reports from these bodies on their work and priorities and look to them for advice when human rights issues within their remit were being considered. If a Human Rights Commission is established in Britain, as in Northern Ireland, then that body should also report to this Parliamentary Committee.

The Human Rights Committee could be innovative in the way that it obtains information and opinions from the public, holding evidence sessions in different parts of the country, as has been suggested by the government, and using less formal procedures when doing so. It must be unrealistic, however, to imagine that the Committee could itself play a major role in raising public awareness of the Act and its implications. The suggestion arose more, one suspects, from a desire to deflect attention from the need for a Human Rights Commission to fulfil that role, than from any real expectation that the committee could do so.

The way in which the Committee would operate in Parliament might be compared with the work of the Public Accounts and Public Administration Committees or the Interdepartmental Environmental Audit Committee. Each is responsible for areas of policy and performance across Whitehall. They investigate matters which could also be of interest to Departmental Select Committees. It will be necessary for the work of the Human Rights Committee to complement the work of those committees, not duplicate them. Although the policy areas investigated by the Human Rights Committee may sometimes fall within the broad remit of an existing Committee, the approach it takes will be quite distinct since its unique mandate will be to investigate compliance with the ECHR and, as suggested by the government itself, with the wider international human rights standards binding on the UK.

The terms of reference for the new Committee, how it is established and approaches its early inquiries will be important for the departmental Select Committees. The Chair will need to liaise closely with chairs of those Committees – perhaps particularly those on Home Affairs, Health, and Education and Employment – where their fields of interest may overlap.

Where a departmental Select Committee is inquiring into an area of policy or practice with a human rights dimension, it should itself consider whether that policy or practice complies with the standards in the ECHR and the UK's wider international human rights obligations. Committee terms of reference may need to be revised so as clearly to permit and encourage this approach.

International treaties

The options for new initiatives, following the Human Rights Act, need not be limited to the scrutiny and monitoring of domestic legislation and policy. If the intention is to enhance Parliament's role in promoting a human rights culture, the government could increase its involvement in the ratification, and monitoring of international human rights treaties.

Government already appears to recognise the former is possible and desirable. It has itself suggested that one of the roles for the new Human Rights Committee might be to:

> examine issues relating to the other international obligations of the United Kingdom such as proposals to accept new rights under other human rights treaties.[32]

In opposition it went further, proposing that the power to ratify treaties should be transferred to Parliament.[33] Parliament is currently permitted only a minimal role in the treaty making process. It is kept in ignorance of much of that process and can be unaware that treaties are being negotiated or about to be ratified. Blackburn points out that Parliamentary approval was not even sought, nor any debate held, when the ECHR was ratified in 1950; this was also the case when the ICCPR was ratified in 1976.[34] In exercise of the prerogative power, the government can agree to treaty obligations which effectively bind Parliament's hands, and do so without effective consultation. Because of this, human rights and freedoms can be, and are, limited by reservations and derogations, depriving citizens of rights intended to be universal in their application, without direct participation by the UK's elected representatives.

Parliament's role in this respect needs to be expanded. Professor Philip Alston of the Australian National University has pointed to the benefits of greater involvement by Parliamentary institutions in their governments' treaty-making. He states:

> ...ensuring Parliamentary participation in the treaty-making process can add transparency and democratic legitimacy while at the same time promoting the goals of efficiency, dependability, and effectiveness in international relations.[35]

The notion that treaty-making is a matter for governments alone is indeed regarded in other European and Commonwealth countries as

outmoded. The majority of EU states involve their legislatures in the
treaty-making process, as do the majority of OECD states.[36]

Some might oppose this approach, arguing that it would risk human
rights standards becoming a hostage to the political fortunes of party
strife in Parliament. However, accepting that potential danger, and
ignoring for the moment straight forward arguments for democratic
accountability, human rights treaties will surely never be prioritised by
MPs and peers whilst these are effectively imposed upon them. If
Parliament is expected to take a closer interest in and concern for human
rights, then the ratification and implementation of international treaties
which bind the UK, should not remain an *exclusively* executive function.

Our recommendations deal with each of the stages of a new
agreement, or amendment to an existing agreement, for example, the
addition of a Protocol.

Negotiation and drafting

The House of Commons Foreign Affairs Select Committee and the
Human Rights Committee should be informed when an international
instrument which has a human rights dimension to it is under
discussion. It would be desirable if not only Parliament but NGOs and
other interested parties were given the opportunity, through timely
briefings, to comment on the approach which the UK might take in the
ensuing negotiations.

Where a major instrument is being negotiated, the Human Rights
Committee may wish to consider the issues in depth, in order to make
considered recommendations to government. It should be informed of
the negotiations to allow it the opportunity to inquire into the issue and
report with recommendations. Whereas the Foreign Affairs Committee
might have views on the implications of the agreement for the situation
in other countries, or for the UK's international relations, the Human
Rights Committee would focus on the implications of the proposed
standards for the UK.

Dossier on new treaties

To aid consultation, the FCO should make available a dossier on
current treaty negotiations, similar to that currently produced by the

Australian Department of Foreign Affairs. This is printed and circulated at least twice a year. All the treaties under negotiation are listed in it, together with a report on their state of progress.

This list should include treaties to which the government is considering becoming a party. Guidelines and other 'soft' law should be included in the list. A synopsis of the measure should be provided and a named contact person responsible for co-ordinating the UK approach, with address, telephone, e-mail and fax numbers given.

Timescale

For human rights treaties, we suggest that a minimum period of two months should elapse between the adoption of the treaty by the relevant international organisation and its signature by the UK government. Once an instrument has been signed by the government, the relevant Parliamentary Committees, NDPBs and NGOs should be notified and the instrument tabled in Parliament together with a statement including the information listed below. A minimum period of three months should then elapse before it can be ratified.

Signature and ratification

For Parliament to be bound into the treaty making process, the ratification of a treaty, convention or binding obligation with an identifiable human rights dimension could be subject to an affirmative procedure similar to that used for a Statutory Instrument. 'Soft' law to which the UK becomes party could be adopted by a 'prayer', or the negative procedure, after it had been laid before Parliament for a period of two months. We suggest that consideration should be given to this approach but recognise that it would raise the broader issue of Parliament's role in relation to international agreements on non-human rights issues.

Information for Parliament

After signature and prior to ratification, we propose that the government should table, with the instrument, a statement including, *inter alia*:

- the terms of the treaty and the obligations it would entail for the UK, including legislative reform

- the anticipated human rights, social and economic impact of the treaty and any consequence there might be were the UK not to ratify it

- the relevance of any subsequent anticipated protocols to the convention

- proposed reservations and/or derogations including reasons for these and their likely duration

- the extent of consultation already carried out with Parliament, NGOs and other interested parties, together with a brief summary of responses received

Parliament should at least have the opportunity to discuss the Treaty before a decision to ratify. In practice, that debate would probably only take place within the Human Rights Committee. It would focus on the implications of the Treaty for the UK, the necessity of any reservations proposed and the extent to which domestic law would need to be amended to bring it into line with the UK's new obligations. Ministers could be questioned on those matters.

New treaties, together with any reservations entered to them, and 'soft' law instruments should be made publicly available. The government is under an obligation to ensure that the public are aware of the UK's obligations under these agreements, with many such agreements having an explicit provision to that effect.

Treaty monitoring

In order to ensure that any new human rights treaty, and the UK's conformity with it, is kept under review we propose that, after the first year, and then at least every five years thereafter, the government should report to the Human Rights Committee on the UK's compliance with the treaty, including the steps which have been taken to reform law, policy or practice to bring them into line with the treaty. This procedure could be timed to coincide with the review of the UK's compliance by the Treaty monitoring body. These reviews normally require the UK to submit a report, at three or five year intervals, reporting its progress in implementing the convention. Lord Lester has, in the past, criticised the failure to consult Parliament prior to submitting these reports.[37]

The Human Rights Act also requires the government to review Reservations and Derogations to Treaties every five years and the Committee is likely to want to be involved in that process.

A 'General Comment' adopted in 1989 by the UN Committee which monitors the ICESCR provides a useful summary of the aims of the UN reporting process. It listed the following:

- To stimulate a comprehensive review of national legislation, administrative rules and procedures as well as government practices and policies for conformity with the treaty. The continuing need and justification for reservations and derogations should also be thoroughly and critically reviewed prior to every subsequent periodic report.

- To ensure regular national monitoring by the government. Domestic monitoring and the regular collection of information can serve to alert Parliament, public bodies, NGOs, the media and the general public to problems and thereby intensify the pressure for change.

- To stimulate the formulation and development of policy.

- To facilitate domestic public scrutiny and government accountability.

- The evaluation of progress towards full implementation and respect for human rights.

- Facing up to problems and shortcomings. Governments are not expected to be perfect but will be heavily criticised for arrogance or complacency and for hiding or glossing over problems and difficulties.

- The exchange of information and experience about methods of human rights observance and protection. The Committee has distilled this collective experience into General Comments or Recommendations which serve as guidelines for all states.[38]

The reporting process has considerable benefits and presents opportunities for a range of public bodies and other organisations to engage with government on improving understanding and respect for human rights in the UK. Alston has referred to the importance of such popular participation in this way:

> ...in situations in which no such discussion has occurred, it is probably safe to assume that the report is either so anodyne and detached as to generate no interest or that the appropriate forums have not been used. Governments should be encouraged to schedule their own reports for debate in the national legislature, for consideration by committees of experts or by nationally active non-governmental groups and should report to the treaty bodies on any such discussions.[39]

What is needed is an approach, and a range of procedures, which ensure that those with an obvious interest in the monitoring process, such as members of both Houses of Parliament, NDPBs and NGOs are engaged and assisted by government to make that process effective.

As a minimum, procedures are now needed to ensure that, when the UK is criticised by a monitoring Committee, Parliament is made aware of this and acts on it, seeking proposals from the government in relation to those matters it accepts and reasons for not acting where it rejects the criticism. This would be an important role for the Human Rights Committee.

The present government has already taken some steps to increase recognition of the UN reporting requirements including the publication of an annual human rights report by the Foreign and Commonwealth Office and Department for International Development. More could be done. Dates and details of the forthcoming reports should, for instance, be listed in the FCO treaties dossier we have proposed, including the contact details of the FCO official responsible.

Although the FCO is responsible for liaising with the UN supervisory body, a separate lead department is likely to compile it. Thus, for instance, the Department of Health compiles the report to the UN Committee on the Rights of the Child (UNCRC). That department should inform the Human Rights Committee of the timetable for producing the report. It should also consult relevant NDPBs and NGOs, as indeed the Department of Health recently did when compiling its second report to the UNCRC.

It should also be possible for the public to obtain a full set of past reports and the summary record of the monitoring committee's proceedings. Departmental libraries should hold copies of the reports and make these available to members of the public wishing to read and photocopy them. Any criticisms of current UK practice contained in those reports should automatically be considered when that area of policy is under review.

At the start of the reporting process the relevant department should publish copies of the convention, the previous report and summary record, making these available free to the public. The departmental library needs to ensure that the House of Commons' and House of Lords' libraries are supplied with all relevant reports.

The Human Rights Committee may use the opportunity provided by the reporting process to hold its own inquiry into the UK's record in relation to that convention. It should be entitled to see a draft of the government's report and might comment or decide to take evidence before doing so. It might then take evidence only or produce a full report with findings and recommendations.

The government's final report should be published as a Command Paper by the Stationery Office and made freely available. Copies should be distributed to all relevant Parliamentary Committees and NDPBs and made available on the internet.

The New Zealand government issues a special publication after each UN examination which contains in one document the government's report, the text of any supplementary written questions and answers, a summary of the oral examination and the text of the Committee's conclusions. This practice was recently strongly commended by the Committee for CERD – the UK government should give serious consideration to adopting it.

When the UN Committee has issued its Conclusions and Recommendations, the government should ensure that Parliament is informed. If criticisms have been made, the Human Rights Committee should hear the Minister's response and details of any reforms proposed. Alternatively, if Ministers reject the Conclusions and Recommendations, then Members of each House should be informed of their full reasons for doing so.

If this might appear too much of a burden on the parliamentary timetable, it should be remembered that these debates would only take place once in every three- or five-year period. In the course of the year to April 1998, for example, only one Periodic Reporting process reached its conclusion, into the UN Covenant on Economic, Social and Cultural Rights. In some years, more than one UN Committee review will be undertaken on the UK. Then, it would be possible for the relevant Reports and Recommendations to be joined and considered together during a single human rights debate.

Human Rights Committee: summary of its functions

In this section, we draw together the roles and responsibilities of the Committee. We then comment on its structure, membership and resources.

The terms of reference establishing the Human Rights Committee should require it to monitor compliance by the UK with the ECHR and with the other international human rights standards binding on the UK. It should monitor the impact of the Human Rights Act and provide Parliament and the government with its opinion on the effectiveness of this legislation and on any changes which may be needed in the Act or its implementation. The committee should take primary responsibility for scrutinising legislation, primary and secondary, for compliance with international human rights standards and in scrutinising existing legislation, policy and practice.

In the absence of a Human Rights Commission in Britain, the Committee could have a role in relation to raising public awareness of those standards and their implications, although in practice parliamentary committees are not well equipped to fulfil such a role. Its role is likely to be limited to monitoring the government's strategy to raise awareness, both among public bodies covered by the Human Rights Act and among the public at large.

The White Paper, *Rights Brought Home*, proposed, as we have, that:

> The new Committee might conduct enquiries on a range of human rights issues relating to the Convention, and produce reports so as to assist the government and Parliament in deciding what action to take. It might also want to range more

widely, and examine issues relating to the other international obligations of the United Kingdom such as proposals to accept new rights under other human rights treaties.[40]

The proposed functions of the Committee could therefore be defined as:

- to scrutinise Bills and secondary legislation for conformity to international human rights standards, particularly the ECHR;

- to consider government proposals for Remedial Orders under the Human Rights Act and review any legislation where Declarations of Incompatiblity have been made;

- to monitor compliance of UK law, policy and practice with human rights standards, including the ECHR, and the adequacy of the machinery for promoting and enforcing those standards;

- to inquire into serious or systematic abuses of human rights;

- to promote public understanding of, and respect for, human rights;

- to provide a forum in which to review the work of the statutory bodies working in the human rights field (for example, CRE, EOC);

- to participate, through consultation, in the process of human rights treaty ratification and amendment;

- to participate in the formal process of monitoring of UK compliance with the human rights treaties by UN committees, the Council of Europe and other international bodies to which the UK is a party.

Status and structure of the Committee

Rights Brought Home stated that:

...in the government's view the best course would be to establish a new Parliamentary Committee with functions relating to human rights. This would not require legislation or any change in Parliamentary procedure. There could be a Joint Committee of both Houses of Parliament or each House could have its own Committee; or there could be a Committee which met jointly for some purposes and separately for others.[41]

There are a few Parliamentary Committees whose membership is made up of members of both Houses. This, as has now been agreed, would be the most suitable model for the Human Rights Committee. Membership is likely to be drawn equally from each of the Houses and the Committee should have the option of creating sub-committees for specific functions. We envisage that it would do so in order to undertake its scrutiny role. The advantages of a joint committee over separate committees are the following:

- Representation from both Houses would reflect the constitutional significance of the Committee's work and enhance its authority, necessary when tackling controversial issues.

- A joint membership would combine the expertise and interest currently found in the House of Lords with the political weight and influence associated with a Commons membership.

- If the Committee is given a scrutiny function then its joint membership would enable a co-ordinated response and remove the possibility of separate Lords and Commons committees reaching different conclusions on the same legislation. This was the main reason that the separate Lords/Commons committees dealing with the scrutiny of Statutory Instruments combined into a Joint Committee. It would also save time.

- A combined Committee would require less resources than those needed to support two committees.

- As recognised by the government, joint membership would not preclude its Lords' and Commons' members from meeting separately for specific purposes should this prove to be necessary or desirable. Blackburn, for instance, suggests that the committee could meet as a joint committee to report on technical matters, such as legislative compliance with the ECHR, where it is important for Parliament to have a single source of authoritative advice, but could conduct separate inquiries into matters of existing policy.[42]

Resources

Apart from the usual resources needed by any Committee of the House, the special nature of its work and the relevance of international jurisprudence would mean that expert legal advice would have to be readily available to members. This is extremely important, particularly in the absence of a Human Rights Commission to provide that service. If a Human Rights Commission is established in Britain it would be able to complement the resources available to the Committee, providing it with data, advice and information which it would otherwise have to obtain itself.

In the course of its investigations and inquiries, we suggest that the Committee make a particular effort to seek the views of those affected by any restrictions on their rights or whose interests are argued in support of these limitations. Members may not only to have to visit, for example, places where people are detained but also hold hearings in which the public can participate and by which the Committee will gain a clear perspective on the relevant social, moral and ethical issues. The Committee may need additional resources to undertake consultation and evidence gathering of this nature. However, the public and the general profile for human rights in society and Parliament will certainly benefit from this more inclusive style of working.

Powers

In order to conduct investigations effectively and to report the Committee would need the same powers as any other Select Committee. For Commons committees, these are currently found in Standing Order 152 and empower a committee:

- to send for persons, papers and records

- to appoint special advisers

- to report

- to communicate their evidence to other committees and the Committee of Public Accounts

- to meet with other committees to take evidence and consider reports

Links with other committees and public bodies

It would not be desirable for the Committee to take over responsibility for *all* human rights concerns and for all aspects of Parliamentary scrutiny. The government's aim is that Parliament as a whole should play a greater role in this field, not only a specialist committee. The work of the Human Rights Committee should be complemented by that undertaken by other Committees. Their significance of human rights principles for the issues they cover should equally be enhanced. The relationship which the Human Rights Committee has with other Committees in the House will help determine its effectiveness and influence; whether or not it becomes a 'ghetto' for human rights issues or a force for change throughout Westminster. As we have noted, the Committee chairs will need to liaise to avoid tension over potentially over-lapping roles, particularly in relation to the inquiry function.

NDPBs with responsibilities for human rights in the field of discrimination and data protection (the EOC, CRE, Data Protection Registrar and the new Disability Rights Commission) could, as we have argued, report to the Human Rights Committee. We envisage this will increase the interest shown by Parliament in the work of these bodies with evidence taken more regularly on the issues of policy and performance raised in their reports. If a Human Rights Commission is created for Britain then we propose that it should report to the Human Rights Committee and that the appointment of its members should be subject to the approval of Parliament. This could be achieved by the Chair of the Human Rights Committee, in addition to the Leader of the Opposition, being involved in the appointment process.

A Human Rights Commission

During the passage of the Human Rights Bill, many Parliamentarians pressed the government to establish an independent Human Rights Commission to monitor and promote awareness of the Act and give assistance to individuals who believe that their rights have been infringed. While the same MPs and peers welcomed the proposal to establish a Parliamentary Human Rights Committee, they argued that, in the words of Lord Simon of Glaisdale:

the functions recommended are entirely different from those
which would concern a parliamentary committee. The two
are complementary.[43]

IPPR has published detailed proposals on the options for such a
body[44] and a Commission has recently been established in Northern
Ireland. The government has not accepted the need for a Human
Rights Commission in Britain, but it has not ruled out the possibility
in the future. It wishes to be clear about the relationship which the
Commission would have with existing bodies, such as the Equal
Opportunities Commission and the Commission for Racial Equality,
that have some responsibility for human rights in the field of equality
and discrimination. The government itself suggested that the
Parliamentary Human Rights Committee should conduct an inquiry
into the need for a Human Rights Commission in Britain and this
responsibility is within its proposed terms of reference.

The Commission's aim would be to promote and protect human
rights, its scope including the international human rights treaties
ratified by the UK. It would provide guidance to public bodies on
their responsibilities under the Human Rights Act, give advice and
assistance to the public, take test cases through the courts and
conduct inquiries. It would also assist with scrutiny of legislation,
making public its opinion on the conformity or otherwise of
legislation to the ECHR. The extent to which it would conduct the
latter role could depend, in part, on the extent to which the
Parliamentary Committee had itself adequate resources to do so.

A Human Rights Commission could therefore greatly assist
Parliament with its work on scrutiny and monitoring. It could become
the eyes and ears of the Human Rights Committee, supplying it with
guidance and evidence in the course of its inquiries.

Conclusion

The Human Rights Act requires the government to improve the scrutiny of
legislation and policy to ensure their compatibility to the European
Convention. But it also presents a challenge to government: whether it
will go further and use the reforms in Whitehall and Parliament to enable
those institutions to foster a culture of rights in every aspect of their work.

The need for new Cabinet Office guidance is already recognised. Such guidance should not be limited merely to compliance, but through the preparation of human rights impact assessments, should ensure that, wherever possible, policy initiatives make a positive contribution to human rights protection. Designating a named Minister to lead on the implementation of this approach, supported by a central unit, Ministerial sponsors within each department and an annual reporting process will help to ensure that this objective is implemented effectively.

The new Parliamentary Human Rights Committee will be established with members from both Houses of Parliament. It should scrutinise primary and secondary legislation for compliance with human rights standards; examine government policy and performance in relation to human rights; conduct inquiries into the adequacy of the arrangements for protecting rights, particularly the effectiveness of the Human Rights Act; monitor the activities and effectiveness of public bodies with responsibilities for human rights; and participate when the UK is involved in human rights treaty negotiations or review.

If these reforms are implemented, then not only will the government and Parliament be acting effectively to ensure compliance of legislation and policy with the ECHR, and with other international human rights standards binding on the United Kingdom, but also to ensure that those principles inform and guide policy at every level.

Endnotes

1. *Rights Brought Home,* op cit
2. Lord Irvine of Lairg, Lord Chancellor, House of Lords Debates, Official Report 3 November 1997, col 1228.
3. The initial recommendations of the Select Committee on the Modernisation of the House of Commons reflect this attitude and show how change does not have to compromise the fair and effective programming of legislation. See Select Committee on Modernisation of the House of Commons (1997) *The Legislative Process* First Report Session 1997-98 HoC 190 TSO.
4. It announced that it would introduce this change in the White Paper *Rights Brought Home* CM 3782 para 3.4, and has done so.
5. *Human Rights in Foreign Policy: guidelines for posts and departments* FCO, March 1998 (not published).
6. See UN Committee on Economic, Social and Cultural Rights

E/C.12/1/Add.19 12 December 1997.

7. *The Green Book: appraisal and evaluation in central government: Treasury Guidance* TSO 1997.

8. *The Better Regulation Guide and Regulatory Impact Assessment* 1998.

9. *Policy Appraisal and Health: a guide from the Department of Health* 1995.

10. *Policy Appraisal for Equal Treatment* guidance reissued in November 1998. Cabinet Office.

11. *Policy Appraisal and the Environment* HMSO 0 11 752487 5 reprinted 1992; and Environmental Appraisal in Government Departments HMSO 0 11 752915 X, 1994.

12. *Policy Appraisal and the Environment: Policy Guidance* DETR, 1998.

13. Cabinet Office (1997) *Your Right to Know* Cm 3818 TSO.

14. See report of the Advisory Group chaired by Professor Crick (1998), *Education for Citizenship and the teaching of democracy in schools* Qualifications and Curriculum Authority, which Education Ministers are currently considering.

15. S.5(1) Human Rights Act 1993.

16. *Rights Brought Home op cit* para 3.5.

17. Canadian Bill of Rights Examination Regulations 1978 and Canadian Charter of Rights and Freedoms Examination Regulations 1985; quoted in Kinley D, (forthcoming 1999),'Parliamentary Scrutiny for Human Rights Compliance: a duty neglected?' in Alston P, *Promoting Human Rights Through Bills of Rights* Oxford University Press.

18. *Op cit* Kinley D (forthcoming 1999)

19. This report would complement the annual report on the UK's contribution to international human rights development now published jointly by the Foreign Office and the Department for International Development. See FCO and DFID (1998) *Human Rights: Annual report on Human Rights* FCO and DFID.

20. Kinley D (forthcoming, 1999) *op cit*

21. Second Reading of the Human Rights Bill, House of Lords, 3 November 1997, col 1234.

22. Third Reading of the Human Rights Bill, House of Commons, 21 October 1998.

23. Second Reading of the Human Rights Bill, House of Commons, 16 February 1998.

24. Parliamentary Question answered by Margaret Beckett, Leader of the House, col 603.

25. Kinley D (forthcoming, 1999) *op cit* and Blackburn R (1998) 'Parliament and Human Rights' in Oliver D and Drewry G *The Law and Parliament* Butterworths, p186.

26. Kinley, D (forthcoming 1999) *op cit*

27. Blackburn R (1999) 'A Parliamentary Committee on Human Rights' in Blackburn R and Plant R, eds *Constitutional Reform, The Labour Government's Constitutional Reform Agenda* Longman, p387-390

28. *Ibid* p380.

29. Denza E 'Parliamentary Scrutiny of Community Legislation'. This article is based on a paper delivered to the Annual Conference of the Statute Law Society held on 3 October 1992.

30. Blackburn R (1999) *op cit* p375.

31. *A New Agenda for Democracy: Labour's proposals for constitutional reform* 1993.

32. *Rights Brought Home op cit* para 3.7.

33. *A New Agenda for Democracy op cit* p33.

34. Blackburn R (1999) *op cit* p376.

35. Alston P, review of *Parliamentary Participation in the Making and Operation of Treaties: a comparative study* in (1995) Australian Yearbook of International Law, p277.

36. Lester A (et al) *Parliamentary Scrutiny of Non-EU Treaties* January 1999. In that memorandum, the authors propose that the House of Lords establish a Treaties committee to report on all proposed non-EU treaties. Should that committee be established, consideration would need to be given to its role in relation to human rights treaties, and to the human rights implications of treaties, relative to the specialised role of the Human Rights Committee.

37. Lester A (1997) 'Taking human rights seriously' in Blackburn R and Busuttil J (eds) *Human Rights for the 21st Century* Pinter, Ch 4.

38. General Comment 1 (1989) contained in UN Document E/1989/22.

39. *Interim Report on Updated Study by Mr Philip Alston* UN Document A/CONF.157/PC.62/Add.11/Rev.1 at para 99. It updated an earlier comprehensive study on the subject and included a set of important recommendations as to how the system should be strengthened and improved.

40. *Rights Brought Home, op cit* para 3.7.

41. *Ibid* paragraph 3.6.

42. Blackburn R (1999) *op cit* p379.

43. Committee stage of the Human Rights Bill, House of Lords, 24 November 1997, col 851.

44. Spencer S and Bynoe I *A Human Rights Commission, the options for Britain and Northern Ireland* (1998) IPPR

APPENDIX
Strasbourg-Proofing: The text of the 1987 Cabinet Office Circular *Reducing the Risk of Legal Challenge*

I. Challenges in the UK Courts

Consultation

1. A ground for judicial review to which the judges appear to be paying particular attention is the lack, or alleged inadequacy, of consultation with those affected by the decision. The risk of challenge on this ground therefore needs to be carefully borne in mind when formulating policy. This does not mean that consultation should always precede a controversial decision; there are bound to be circumstances where consultation is not possible or desirable if a decision is to be implemented quickly and effectively. In deciding whether to consult, departments should consider whether consultation is required by legislation and, if it is not, whether it has been undertaken in the past or whether there is a legitimate expectation of it. In deciding to proceed without full consultation, Ministers need to have had drawn to their attention any heightened risk of legal challenge that may result.

Preparation of legislation

2. The risk of challenge to administrative action can be reduced if the legislation governing that action is expressed in the clearest possible language, even at the cost of drafting in terms that are presentationally or politically unattractive. The courts are reluctant to go against something which is clearly the express wish of Parliament, and making decisions subject to Parliamentary procedure may therefore be an important safeguard. They will also be influenced in their decisions by such factors as the provision in legislation of avenues of appeal for those affected. Again, there are no hard and fast rules in these areas; but the possibility of reducing the risks of challenge in these ways is a factor which Ministers will need to weigh

when making decisions on the shape of legislation, and departments should ensure that it is drawn to their attention.

3. Proposals for legislation should be scrutinised for likely subjects of challenge. Since the source of challenge to legislative provisions often lies in opposition to the provision on policy grounds, prompting a minute examination of the drafting of the legislation, the lead in departmental scrutiny of draft Bills must come from Ministers and their policy advisers. It is for them to alert their legal advisers and Parliamentary Counsel to those aspects of the policy which are liable to be principally opposed, so that the draftsman can focus on the likely areas of technical challenge. In case of difficulty legal advisers should (following the usual principles concerning the reference of questions to the Law Officers) seek the Law Officers' advice, and should do so as early as possible in the drafting process.

Vetting of draft legislation by outside counsel

4. Where there is a history of legal challenges being mounted in a particular area, there may be advantage in having draft legislation seen by an outside Counsel expert in that field. A department wishing to follow that course should consult the draftsman and the Law Officers' Department or, in respect of Scotland, the Lord Advocate's Department.

Cabinet documents

5. Memoranda submitted to a Cabinet Committee seeking policy decisions should draw attention to any perceived risks of legal challenge. Memoranda accompanying Bills submitted to Legislation Committee should draw attention to any steps taken to reduce the risk of legal challenge.

II. The European Convention on Human Rights

Introduction

6. The UK has been a party to the European Convention on Human Rights (TS No 71 of 1953, Cmnd 8969) since 1951, and is

also a party to several of the Protocols to it. Since 1966 the UK has accepted the right of individuals claiming to be victims of a violation of the Convention by the UK to make direct application to the European Commission of Human Rights. The government is obliged to give effect to judgements of the European Court of Human Rights and decisions of the Committee of Ministers concerning violations by the United Kingdom. Important changes in law and practice have been required as a result. The main rights and freedoms protected concern, briefly: life, torture and inhuman and degrading treatment or punishment; liberty and security (ie freedom from wrongful arrest and detention); fair trial; private and family life; home and correspondence; religion; expression and information; peaceful assembly and association; marriage; property; education; and free elections. Most of the rights permit certain exceptions. There is much case-law of the Commission and Court interpreting the Convention – often on the basis of its purposes rather than literally – and a consistently high level of applications and decisions concern the UK. The Convention has been held to apply in areas where it might not have been initially considered eg school corporal punishment and aircraft noise. Questions on it can sometimes arise in most of the areas of law administered by departments.

Preparation of legislation and administrative measures

7. It *should be* standard practice when preparing a policy initiative for officials in individual departments, in consultation with their legal advisers, to consider the effect of existing (or expected) ECHR jurisprudence on any proposed legislative or administrative measure. Wherever possible, officials should at this stage alert any other departments likely to be affected by the initiative in a similar way. If departments are in any doubt about the likely implications of the Convention in connection with any particular measure, they should seek ad hoc guidance from the Foreign and Commonwealth Office. This request for advice should always be copied to the Law Officers' Department, the Lord Advocate's Department, the Home Office, the Scottish Home and Health Department and the Northern Ireland Office.

Cabinet documents

8. Any memoranda submitted to a Cabinet committee, or accompanying a Bill submitted to Legislation Committee, should include an assessment of impact, if any, of the European Convention on Human Rights on the action proposed (much as Departments already do for European Community implications).

Settlement of cases

9. Where applications to the ECHR have been referred to the government and there is a serious risk of an adverse finding by the Commission or Court, departments should give early consideration to the possibility of friendly settlement if this seems likely to offer a less damaging outcome. The Convention expressly provides for settlement to be considered after the Commission's decision on admissibility, but it is possible at any stage, including during proceedings before the Court (in the nature of things, however, friendly settlement will not in practice be available where an application has been brought as a test case in order to get a ruling from the Court). Before a friendly settlement is offered in Strasbourg, the responsible department must ensure that other departments which will be affected by the outcome of the case are given sufficient opportunity to comment.

Existing measures

10. Although it is not intended that departments should conduct a systematic retrospective look at all existing measures, they should nevertheless consider whether action is needed on existing measures where it is clear that there is a serious risk of an adverse finding at Strasbourg which will affect them.